Brain Injured Children ; - Tapping the Potential Within.

For Daniel, who is sorely missed.

Brain Injured Children. - Tapping the Potential Within

Andrew Brereton

Published by Andrew Brereton. England. 2009

Contents

Introduction

If you are reading this book, your child has probably received a diagnosis of cerebral palsy, autism, dyspraxia, AD(H)D, developmental delay, learning difficulties, epilepsy or any other such term, which essentially means they have brain dysfunction or a brain-injury which has caused neuro – developmental problems. You will understandably be distressed by this; - You are also likely to be suffering from shock, confusion, bewilderment and even anger. These feelings will eventually pass, (apart from the bewilderment, which from personal experience is likely to remain). I speak from the experience of being a parent to a child who suffered profound brain-injuries. Speaking personally, although I have gained qualifications based in neuroscience and child development and studied in many clinics internationally, which offer many varied forms of treatment, my own child remains my most astute tutor, (as your children will be to you). All I have learned and experienced during this time has led me to a greater understanding of the immense difficulties faced by children who suffer from neuro - developmental difficulties and their families.

Any developmental disability is a formidable enemy. If it is unchallenged, it prevents the development of the child's functional capability, eats away at the family's sovereignty and in some cases is a constant threat to the child's health and well-being. Fortunately, this situation does not need to remain unchallenged as there is a wealth of knowledge available, which can be utilised to assist your child's development.

There exists voluminous evidence that the brain possesses a high degree of plasticity. – What does this mean? Well, it means that brain cells are able to change their function or organisation due to environmental experience. (Casasanto, 1998). This means, if we are able to provide the child with an environment, which has the optimum level of stimulation within it, we should be able to stimulate his development. Indeed, the work of researchers such as Kolb (1995), demonstrates very clearly that the brain retains a high degree of plasticity, not only throughout young life, but well into old age!

This moves us to a principle of treatment; - The provision of a developmental environment designed to stimulate and to maximise neural plasticity!

This book has a sharp focus. It is intended as an initial guide to parental understanding; - and with this in mind I have attempted to keep technical language to a minimum. However, sometimes this is impossible and so where I have been forced to use technical language, I have gone to great lengths to provide explanations.

I know from personal experience that what parents need is clear, concise information, (as free as possible of technical jargon), which strikes home as true as the truest arrow.

Another reason for writing the book is to raise awareness of my child development consultancy called 'Snowdrop.' The idea of Snowdrop is that families who are not satisfied with the developmental progress, which their child is currently achieving, can access treatment designed to maximise that progress. This comes in the form of a prescription of a programme of developmental activities, which can be carried out at home.

The book has attempted to achieve a situation, where it examines brain-injury / dysfunction and its major effects upon child development and presents the information in a clear, accessible and informative manner. I have attempted to pull together the best ideas from various systems of treatment and present them alongside my own theories, in an attempt to improve children's developmental prospects and in turn help the families involved. My rationale regarding treatment has been developed from the work of several eminent psychologists / neurologists of the past and a few of the present day. I hope I have achieved my aim.

A definition of terms

Before I begin, allow me to define my terms of reference, I am interested and this book is concerned with children whose development has been affected by brain injury or if you prefer, brain dysfunction. What do I mean by these terms? I mean any variable whether genetic or environmental which causes either structural damage to, or the abnormal functioning of the brain.

There are many things which can cause a brain to malfunction. One involves a genetic explanation. The expression of specific genes can cause the brain to develop and function in a manner which we would not consider to be normal. We know this because we now have evidence that the interplay between genetic expression and the child's developing neurology can in certain individuals, cause specific parts of the brain to wire themselves together differently. A good example of this is seen in some children who have autism.

In the largest genetic study of autism ever attempted — involving more than 3,000 participants from AGRE, (Autism Genetic Resource Exchange) 1,453 cases from other sources and over 7,000 additional control subjects — genetic variations were identified in a region of chromosome 5 that appears to play a pivotal role in about 15% of cases of autism. What makes this region particularly fascinating is that it seems to regulate gene-coding for proteins that are essential to forming connections in the brain (http://www.time.com/time/health/article/0,8599,1894409,00.html)

In another study, using functional magnetic resonance imaging, a team of researchers affiliated with the University of Washington's Autism Centre found that the most severely socially impaired subjects in the study exhibited the most abnormal pattern of connectivity among a network of brain regions involved in face processing.

"This study shows that these brain regions are failing to work together efficiently," said Natalia Kleinhans, a research assistant professor of radiology and lead author of the paper published in the journal 'Brain.' "Our work seems to indicate that the brain pathways of people with autism are not completely disconnected, but they are not as strong as in people without autism."

The study is the first to look at brain connectivity and social impairment, and focused on how the brain processes information about faces. Deficits in face processing are one of the earliest characteristics to emerge in people with autism.

So, we know that the expression of certain genes can lead to the brain adopting an incorrect wiring plan, leading to some of the deficits we see in autism. This is not to say however, that all cases of autism or other neuro - developmental problems have a genetic cause, - indeed they do not! It is also not the case that because the expression of certain genes has caused the brain to wire together incorrectly, that nothing can be done about that! Genes are only activated in response to the presence of the correct external or indeed internal physiological environment. Therefore if we change that environment to a developmentally enriched one, not only do we have the opportunity to harness the inherent plasticity of the brain to re-wire itself, - which is proven to be possible, we might also be able to influence genetic expression!

The other major cause of a brain malfunctioning is a structural injury to the brain, whether that injury is caused by oxygen starvation at birth, poor conditions during pregnancy, infection, malnutrition, exposure to drugs or other toxins, exposure to an impoverished environment, or a thousand other causes. Brain injury may also occur due to a head injury. So a brain may malfunction and consequently the child may experience a developmental disability due to many causes. The developmental disabilities therefore are symptoms of a malfunctioning brain, whether that malfunctioning has a genetic cause or an environmental one, I feel that the term 'brain injury' is a far more accurate description in either case.

What does brain injury do? It produces as symptoms, developmental disabilities in children. There are many varied labels for and definitions of developmental disabilities, probably more than there are developmental disabilities themselves.

Indeed, it seems that even one child can have several developmental disabilities at the same time! For instance, my own child was variously labelled as 'cerebral palsied,' ' autistic,' 'spastic,' 'quadriplegic,' 'epileptic,' 'learning disabled,' ' microcephalic,' 'mentally retarded' and 'athetoid.'

Nine separate diagnoses, - not bad for one child! Now did my son really have those nine crippling conditions? I am not so sure. You see all of those conditions could be viewed as symptoms of an overriding cause, - they are all symptoms produced by his 'brain injury.' What we really need to remember is that they are indeed just symptoms and whilst it is necessary sometimes to pay attention to symptoms (such as in the case of epilepsy), we must not allow these symptoms to distract us from treating their cause, - the brain – injury itself, because if we are successful in doing so, the symptoms will spontaneously improve!

Disclosure of Diagnosis

When a child is born into a family, it is usually a time of great joy and optimism. It is a time when the family looks forward to the future with the shared anticipation of seeing that child take his first steps, speak his first words and hopefully to grow up to fulfil all of the ambitions, of which the composite members of his family could only dream. Most people cannot even imagine the horror of being informed that their child is different; - their child has problems. They cannot imagine the trauma of being informed that he will not pass the milestones, which other children so easily pass; he will not achieve what comes so easily to others. There is no doubt that this is a harrowing experience. At some point in the past, whether recent or distant, you will probably have experienced or know someone who has experienced the horror of this situation. I personally experienced it twenty - four years ago when a consultant paediatrician calmly announced that my son would suffer severe cerebral palsy for the rest of his life, before coolly ushering us out of his office. We travelled home and looked up the meaning of cerebral palsy in a medical dictionary! Now, you would no doubt just 'Google' it, but should you have to? Why should you be treated in this way?

When one considers the devastation, which the deliverance of news such as this can cause, one would imagine parents would be informed as tactfully and discretely as possible. One would also hope parents would be informed together, in warm, hospitable surroundings and be given as much time as necessary to absorb the magnitude and complexity of the information. This certainly does not seem to be the experience of many parents and to this date, there are many research articles in the literature, which demonstrate the disclosure of such diagnosis by medical professionals to be an on-going difficulty.

One mother related a particularly bad example of how the 'news' was broken to her when she explained to me;

"We were sitting in the paediatrician's office and I asked his opinion of Ryan's progress. He just sat there with a cold expression and said; - 'I'm afraid Ryan is showing early signs of having cerebral palsy. I'll see you in one month's time.' – With that we were asked to leave."

Another mother described to me the way in which she was informed about her little girl's problems.

"The best thing you can do is to take her home, keep her warm and comfortable and try to have a proper baby next time."

Out of the myriad of parents to whom I have spoken down the past few years, only once have I ever met parents who were satisfied with the way in which this situation was handled. These assertions are supported by voluminous research dating from the 1960's right through to the present day.

A system, which leaves a delicate task, such as this, to people who are trained to be cold, calculating clinicians, when precisely the opposite traits are required, is seriously flawed. Would it not be more appropriate in such a situation to have someone available who is not such a 'cool, calculating clinician,' someone who ***is*** trained to deal with people on a more human level, who could deliver the news in a more tactful manner? The professional resource is certainly available to do this and utilising it would save parents from having to deal with the trauma of receiving such shocking news, delivered in such a dreadfully incompetent manner. Psychologists and other counselling professionals abound and are qualified to deal with every conceivable stressful situation. This professional resource should be tapped, with experienced professionals on hand to talk parents through this dreadfully sensitive situation and beyond. They should act as the parent's 'advocate' with the medical profession and as such would be in a position to provide first-hand information and support to new parents. They would be able to guide the family through the emotional minefield, which is to come.

Bringing such a system into the 'front line' instead of tolerating a situation where overwrought, confused parents have to find information and access to support services on their own would eradicate other difficulties.

- Many parents who are dissatisfied with the explanations and information concerning their child's problems, given to them by the doctor (and there are many!), might be satisfied.

- Input from various disciplines could be more accurately tailored to parental need.
- Parents would be more expertly guided through the trauma of coming to accept their child's problems, than they ever could be by someone whose training was purely clinical.

Will the medical profession heed these words? No! I predict that parents will still be voicing the same complaints in twenty years' time.

Reaction and Adjustment

It is recognised by most parents and professionals with whom I have spoken, that there are definite reaction stages, through which most parents pass after the discovery of their child's disabilities. I have no doubt you will, or already have experienced the same process. I know I did!

The initial reaction, as it was in my own case, after the diagnosis of my son, is usually one of shock, followed by reactions such as disbelief, anger, confusion and even guilt. In my own individual research down the years, I have consulted many parents concerning their feelings during this initial period. All of them without exception confirmed reactions similar to those described above.

This period of confused emotion is usually closely followed by grief, as parents mourn the loss of the child, which 'should have been.' This may seem a strange concept to the outsider, but the child, which has been nurtured for nine months inside his mother's womb, is simply no more. Instead he has been replaced by another child, - one with terrible problems. To many parents, it is as though a child has died. One mother I know pointed this out to me very succinctly;

"The little girl I had carried for nine months had gone. I felt I had come to know her and then she had died. I was left looking after a stranger."

These feelings are sometimes very strong and can cause serious problems for families, who find it difficult to relate to and bond with the new arrival. These thoughts and emotions are usually underrated by medical professionals and in the vast majority of cases little support or counselling seems to be offered. Families are left to their own devices as they desperately attempt to come to terms with the enormity of their child's problems. It is here that further developmental complications can arise as normal interaction patterns between parents and child fail to develop, - a situation which compromises the development of language and communication.

It is now that parents seem to branch into two readily identifiable categories as follows.

The conformists. These parents appear to fall into three further sub-categories.

- Parents who believe their child needs love and protection and anything, which goes beyond this, is not even to be considered. As one mother stated. *"We think any kind of stimulation would be cruel, we don't want anything like that."* I place no criticism or judgement on this point of view, I understand it completely.

- Parents who appear to have been programmed into believing that the doctor is always right and consequently they are only open to this single channel of information. The problem is, this channel of information can be as unreliable as any other! I recall when my wife and I were considering taking our son for treatment to the Peto Institute in Hungary. A doctor visiting our home, whose field was child development, tried in the most intolerable way to discourage my wife from taking this entirely reasonable course of action by saying; - *"I would consider Hungary very carefully if I were you, after all you will be away from home for several months. Whilst you are away, your husband could quite easily move someone else in!"*

- The third subgroup of the conformists is the 'reluctant accepters.' These are the parents who are interested in exploring every possibility, which may be utilised to help their children, but are constrained by some circumstance, which is outside their control from doing so.

The non-conformists. – These parents are the ones who are likely to pursue other possibilities of treatment for their children and they appear to fall into two further subgroups.

- Parents who have not completely adjusted to their child's problems and are determined, (sometimes unrealistically), to disprove all the experts who have written off their child. These parents unfortunately have not made it to the final stages of adjustment to their child's problems. Again, I do not criticise them, because I was once one of their number!

- Parents, who have adjusted well to their child and his problems and despite all of the adverse medical 'opinion,' see no harm in exploring all possibilities, which may help their child. (And there will be adverse opinion, simply because you will be exploring strategies for treatment, which are outside the realms of medicine: - many medical people will perceive this as some sort of threat).

OK, so you have probably fallen into one of the above categories and you have decided which course of action, (or inaction) you are going to embark upon. This is entirely your choice and no one has the right to be critical of you whatever that choice may be.

How can a brain – injury affect my child?

A brain – injury / dysfunction is as individual as a fingerprint. Yes, when specific parts of the brain become injured, predictable sets of symptoms arise, that is why we are able to label groups of children as having cerebral palsy, or autism, or as having other neurodevelopmental disorders. However the precise pattern and severity of injury is different in each child, which is why the precise nature of the problems faced by each child is unique.

There are several major areas of development, visual, auditory, tactile, cognitive, hand function, mobility, language and socialisation. A brain injury / dysfunction can affect one or any number of these areas in differing degrees of severity in individual children. Some children might be profoundly affected in many or all areas and consequently be dependent upon their parents for every aspect of their physical care. Some might be only slightly affected in one or more areas. The common factor is that they both have brain – injuries / dysfunctions and I think this terminology is preferable because it is simpler and more accurate.

Let us take a look at each major area of development and highlight some of the difficulties which can be caused for our children.

Visual problems

Many people regard vision as their most important sense. I would agree and the neurology seems to support this view. 25% of the human cortex is devoted to processing visual information. With that huge amount of cortex devoted to just one sense, the chances are that any diffuse brain-injury will knock out a significant portion of brain cells dedicated to vision. Is it surprising therefore, that so many of our children experience visual difficulties? Also, one of the first areas of the brain to be injured through oxygen starvation is the thalamus, an important area for relaying incoming sensory information to the cortex.

If visual development is affected then the child can experience difficulties in the areas of language, socialisation and mobility development, as they form the sensory and motor parts of 'input – output loops' respectively. Some of the vital precursors of language and social development involve the use of vision in order to make eye – contact, to learn to look at faces and to learn to share and regulate mutual attention with an interacting partner. The implications for the effect of lack of visual ability for the development of mobility are obvious for all to see as the motivation to move would be impaired as would the safety of movement.

Sometimes the visual system of the child might be knocked out completely. In these cases, there is nothing wrong with the eyes; it is just that the child's neuro - visual system is not responding to the visual signal from the environment. This is called ***'cortical visual impairment,' (CVI) or 'cortical blindness.'*** The child's pupils may dilate and contract normally and eye movements might also seem normal and indeed it is rare, (although it does happen), for a child to have no vision at all. It is more of a case of an inconsistent visual response, the vision sometimes seeming to be switched on and sometimes switched off. Many children who have other developmental problems also suffer cortical visual impairment.

I remember one little boy I treated, who was totally unresponsive in visual terms. He did possess a pupillary light reflex, (his pupils dilated when in the dark and constricted when in the light). His doctors, who had informed the parents that he was probably neurologically blind, were not doing anything to try to remedy the situation. It took the parents two years of patiently stimulating their son's visual development under my direction, to bring his vision to a level where he would visually track an object across a room and visually explore his environment. The most moving moment however, was the first time he looked his mother in the eye and smiled. From there, I instituted further stimulation, which later culminated in the adoption of a reading programme. He made incredible progress!

Another neuro – visual problem is that the child might process visual stimulation in a distorted manner. Such a distortion would be an inability to focus visual attention on a particular feature of the environment, which would mean that all aspects of the visual environment were competing for attention simultaneously. Such ***wide spectrum tuning*** of visual attention would also create a situation where the child would not have the ability to 'tune out' some elements of the visual field. The consequence of this is chaos for the children who suffer this problem, causing anxiety and high stress.

This type of visual over-sensitivity was reported by Bruno (2006), who endured brain-injury through a car accident. She described how brain-injury propelled her into a world of psychological perplexity, double vision and incapacitating visual and auditory over-sensitivity

Many parents report that the visual world is just too much for their children, indeed children have themselves reported a situation where they are unable to focus on a single visual stimulus. It seems that apart from inappropriate activity from the brain's attentional mechanisms, damage to parts of the brain's ***parietal lobes*** can lead to this type of visual difficulty. A child may appear to be competently scanning his visual environment, but cannot attend to particular visual features of that environment! (Carlson, 2007).

The child who suffers this problem is only truly at peace when he is asleep. He rarely makes eye-contact, because he has difficulty attending to the single visual stimulus of the eyes, which are competing with other visual stimuli in the environment (does this ring any bells for parents of children diagnosed with autism?). Everything is competing for his visual attention simultaneously, so he finds it impossible to focus on any one person or object. As a consequence of his inability to cope with his visual world, the child with this problem can, in a desperate measure to protect his immature, overwhelmed sensory system, 'withdraw' into himself.

Another distortion of visual processing is a visual attentional system which is too narrowly focussed. This ***narrow visual tuning*** produces an effect where the child appears not to be aware of most of his visual environment, singling out one object and almost completely focussing his attention on it. This 'over-focussed' attention can appear to be obsessive behaviour to the outsider. This child plays with one toy and one toy only because he is focussed upon specific features of it. He may be fascinated with movement, such as a spinning top, or wheels moving and will spend hours just looking at this.

Rizzo & Robin, (1990), describe this situation perfectly. Apart from a malfunctioning neurological tuning mechanism, injuries to the ***parietal lobes*** of both hemispheres of the brain can also create a situation whereby individuals can only pay visual attention to one object at a time. This is known as ***Balint's syndrome*** and it is possible that some of our children, who experience 'narrow visual tuning' difficulties, will have injuries in this part of the brain.

However, there is also an alternative and convincing developmental explanation for 'narrow visual tuning.' Young babies have difficulty in transferring their attention; - this is well known and is a developmental phase. Infants who are less than four months of age will sometimes stare at an attractive object, being unable to transfer their gaze. Occasionally this inability to displace their visual attention will make them cry out in distress (Johnson et al, 1991). It could very well be that some children, who have 'narrow visual tuning' difficulties, never emerge from this phase of visual development.

Some children experience a type of visual over-sensitivity whereby the sensory tuning system of the child is acting to amplify the visual information, which the eyes are taking in. The child, who suffers such ***visual over-amplification*** problems, is the child who hates bright lights. He particularly dislikes sunny days and hates anything moving close to his eyes.

He may not concentrate on anything at all with his central vision, preferring to view things from the less threatening position of his peripheral vision. We, as healthy individuals are allowed a small insight into the way this child feels when we have a migraine attack and our vision becomes sensitive to bright lights. What is occurring both in migraine sufferers and with our brain-injured children is that specific inhibitory systems of the tuning system within the brain are not activated sufficiently, resulting in overstimulation in the visual cortex. (Mulleners et al, 2001).

Unfortunately, this is the visual world, which this child inhabits 24/7. This child will not make eye contact, but for different reasons to the child with wide spectrum tuning difficulties; - this child literally finds eye contact to be very threatening and will avoid the situation at all costs.

Some children experience the exact opposite of this problem in that the sensory tuning system of the brain is simply not exciting the cortex sufficiently and so it is unable to process incoming sensory information. These children, who are experiencing ***visual under-amplification,*** are sun–worshippers; they find bright lights and visually attractive displays to be absolutely fascinating. Children with this problem, if their motor control allows, can often be found waving their hands in front of their eyes in an attempt to self - stimulate their visual system.

Children showing under-amplification problems, like those displaying over-amplification difficulties can seem hard to reach, but for the opposite reason; - they are simply not processing visual information from the visual world around them.

A final distortion of sensory processing in the visual system is that of ***internal tuning.*** In this phenomenon the visual system is tuned inwardly to visual phenomena, which it itself is creating. Again, it is possible to relate this to what happens to certain individuals who suffer from migraine. Many migraine sufferers, (including myself!), experience a 'visual display' prior to an attack, where all sorts of shapes and colours occlude the vision. Similarly, the visual system of some brain–injured children is capable of producing this effect. These children appear preoccupied with looking at something, which cannot be determined! They appear to be staring into the mid–distance and it can be immensely difficult to break their concentration. As early as 1956, Beck and Guthrie were describing the internally generated visual phenomena experienced by individuals who had suffered brain-injuries, one describing seeing different coloured orbs in their visual field, floating up and down. (p. 6). Is it any wonder that some of our children are fixated upon this self – generated visual world?

Other visual problems

The development of vision and the child's ability to use his visual skills in a meaningful way may be, as I have just described, distorted by brain-injury or brain dysfunction. Visual development therefore will most likely be stopped, or slowed to snail's pace. Injury may interfere with the smooth operation of the visual pathways in the brain, or cause direct injury to part of the brain known as the ***occipital cortex***, which is the processing centre for vision. Injuries such as these can take a terrible toll. They can take the visual ability of the child back to pre-birth stages.

Other visual problems, sustained by brain-injured children include visual field problems; - Each hemisphere of the brain is responsible for processing visual information from one half of the visual field, (the opposite side), so an injury to part of the occipital cortex in the right hemisphere of the brain can cause a visual deficit in the left visual field and injury to part of the left occipital cortex can cause deficits to the right visual field.

Another phenomenon, which can occur due to injury to the occipital cortex, is that the child may not notice movement within his visual environment. He may pay good visual attention to most aspects of his visual environment and yet fail to detect the sudden movement of an object close by.

Deficits in the ability to perceive colour (***cerebral achromatopsia***), may also be experienced due to brain-injury. Interestingly, this problem may occasionally be experienced in only one half of the visual field, if the injury to this part of the occipital cortex is only in one hemisphere. Patients with this type of injury in both hemispheres report their vision as being in black and white. (Heywood & Kentridge, 2003).

Other common visual symptoms often experienced as a consequence of brain injury are:

- Double vision
- Difficulties with moving gaze quickly from one point to the other. (saccadics),
- Focusing difficulties.
- Binocular vision (eye alignment)

This is by no means an exhaustive taxonomy of neuro-visual problems, - just a list of the most common difficulties experienced by our children.

Auditory Problems

Auditory development, as the term suggests, is vital for the development of our ability to hear and consequently the development of the ability to understand and produce language. Without hearing, language development is severely affected, as they are the sensory and motor parts of an 'input – output loop' respectively. With distorted auditory development, language development is often itself distorted. We will now consider the ways in which distorted auditory development can affect the child. As with cortical visual impairment, the brain injury can totally impair the child's hearing, creating a cortical deafness, otherwise known as central hearing loss. Children who have a wide range of developmental problems also suffer cortical deafness

Evidence has accrued over many years, which suggests that the brain extensively analyses sounds to which we are apparently not paying attention. However, having analysed these sounds within our environment, part of the brain decides that the vast majority of them are unimportant, so they receive no further processing and no further attentional resources are diverted towards them. In other words, we actively 'filter out' sounds, which our attentional systems consider to be unimportant. So what happens when a child who has suffered brain-injuries loses the ability to focus his hearing and to filter out sounds efficiently?

Auditory ***wide spectrum tuning*** is one of the most difficult problems a child and a family can face. Children with this problem experience difficulties in devoting attentional resources to sounds to which they need to pay attention and conversely have difficulties in 'filtering out' sounds to which they do not need to pay attention. Simply, the brain is attempting to devote attentional resources to everything in the auditory environment. To understand this, imagine yourself seated in your lounge, having a conversation with a friend. You have no difficulty in attending to your friend and what she has to say. A car passes by the window whilst you are talking and you completely ignore it, you may not even be aware that it has happened; you have successfully 'tuned out' the sound of the car and selectively paid attention to what your friend was saying.

In sharp contrast however, the attentional and filtering system of the child with brain-injury may not be able to succeed in accomplishing this sophisticated task. Because of the breakdown in his ability to filter out non-important sounds, his system attempts to attend to everything simultaneously! – All noise in the environment is concurrently competing for his attention. He must live in a world of unimaginable chaos!

Children who experience this type of difficulty can understandably present as being hyper-anxious and agitated. The child may withdraw completely into himself as a necessary defensive strategy in order to try to escape a chaotic world. Many of these problems have the 'knock on' effect of slowing or completely stopping the language development of a child, as he cannot separate the speech sounds of the human voice from all other background noise.

I will never forget the state of one little chap whose parents brought him to see me. They wheeled him into the room and I knew instantly what his major problem was; - he was experiencing sensory overload. His muscle tone was rigid, his breathing was strained and anxious and he was obviously ***very*** aware (too aware) of everything which was happening around him. I privately wondered how the child managed to survive each day. I informed the parents that in my opinion, the 'tuning system' in their son's brain was malfunctioning and in particular his brain was attempting to process too much of the auditory stimuli in the environment. To prove my point, I made sure the general noise level was reduced and asked that we should all lower our speaking voice to a whisper. Within a few minutes, the child was much calmer. I recommended a programme of sound reduction, auditory training and vestibular stimulation, which had the effect of further calming the young man.

Human beings have an amazing capability to focus auditory concentration, (this is particularly the case concerning spoken language), to the utterance of one specific speaker who may be talking within the noise created by a loud group of people. Recordings of brain activity with positron emission topography (PET), advocate that a complicated set of connections, which comprises several brain regions, (auditory, frontal and parietal areas of the cortex), are involved in our ability to selectively attend to a single auditory signal in this way, (Sinkkonen &Tervaniemi, 2000).

In the child who suffers ***narrow spectrum tuning*** difficulties, this ability is too efficient and he over-focuses his attention and has difficulty widening that attention to incorporate other salient features of his auditory environment. Outwardly, his behaviour can easily cause him to be confused with the child who suffers 'under-amplification' difficulties. His tuning system only allows him to attend to one stimulus at a time and so he can give the impression of being under-sensitive to all other sounds in his environment. This child, in his attention to sound, can appear to obsess on one particular feature of the environment to the exclusion of all else.

Haist et al, (2005), in their research on specific types of brain-injury and its effect upon the individual's attention, point to the fact that certain patterns of injury have a tendency to produce an attentional system which over-focuses. These findings corroborate my own experience in dealing with children who face these difficulties.

Another distortion of auditory processing concerns children, who experience ***auditory under-amplification*** difficulties. These children love loud noises. I knew one child who, if an air horn was used right next to him, would react with pure delight. (Please do not try this until you have ensured that your child definitely suffers under-amplification problems by having him professionally evaluated). Children who experience this problem can become very frustrated as they desperately attempt to make as much noise as possible in order to self–stimulate their auditory system.

In the case of children such as this, the brain's sensory tuning system, (the thalamus, limbic system and reticular formation), is not exciting the cortex sufficiently to allow it to process sensory stimulation from the environment. It is also the case, as it is with their over-sensitive counterparts, that some of these children are selectively under sensitive to particular frequencies. This will be reflected in their language development, as they will have difficulty in receiving, processing and consequently producing specific speech sounds.

At the other end of the spectrum, the world is simply too loud and oppressive a place for children who experience ***auditory over-amplification*** difficulties. Every sound seems amplified. Children with this problem can occasionally appear not to be hearing anything, as they 'close down' the threat of the auditory world. They simply cannot deal with a world, which is too loud and threatening.

Children who suffer auditory over-amplification difficulties may react badly to hearing specific frequencies to which they may be sensitive, or they may demonstrate a generalised over-sensitivity. They also fare badly in acoustically unfriendly places such as bathrooms. I worked with one child who would scream hysterically every time his parents used the vacuum cleaner, to the point where the parents were forced to take him out of the house when it needed to be used. Other children I have known have demonstrated sensitivity to high-pitched noises and demonstrated some quite unusual reactions to them. I know one little chap who 'giggles' every time he hears a whistling sound, which sounds amusing, but this is no 'giggle' of enjoyment, it was an involuntary reaction and if you looked into his eyes you would know instantly that it is false and that the noise is actually causing him pain. It was later discovered that the reaction this child was producing to sound was in fact a type of epileptic reaction known as 'gelastic epilepsy.'

Some recent research has also linked this type of sensory over-stimulation difficulty to an under-production of a chemical called ***5-hydroxytryptamine***, a precursor to ***serotonin***, (Marriage, 1995). This would support my observations, which connect children's sensory over-sensitivities with the development of a poor sleeping pattern, (correct serotonin levels are also necessary for the smooth operation of the sleep / wake cycle).

One little girl who I was privileged enough to see, clearly suffered problems of auditory over-amplification. To the untrained eye she seemed passive enough, sitting in her chair apparently at peace, (she was actually 'closed down,' trying to keep a distance from the threatening world around her). There were however little tell-tale signs that she was not at peace and as I observed her I formed the conclusion that she may in fact be over-amplifying. To test out this hypothesis I took a tuning fork and gently tapped it on the edge of the desk. Her reaction was immediate and startling: - She screamed in pain!

The final distortion of auditory processing I wish to discuss is ***internal auditory tuning***. Ever hear the old saying, 'I've got bells in my ears?' Anyone who has experienced this phenomenon for a while, will comprehend a little of what these children have to endure. - People who suffer from 'tinnitus' certainly will understand. This child cannot focus on the outside world, because his tuning system is forcing the cerebral cortex to attend to the noise, which his own sensory system is producing. He can appear to be barely aware of what is occurring around him. He may be intently listening to his own internal sounds, such as the pulse of blood being pumped through his ears, or his sensory system may be producing its own auditory ***white noise*** on which he is fixated. Many authors term this phenomenon an ***auditory aura,*** which emanates from injury to or over-excitation of the ***primary auditory cortex.*** Hughlings – Jackson first connected the auditory aura to a specific type of epilepsy known as ***Jacksonian*** epilepsy.

Hughlings-Jackson described three cases of the auditory aura, which he integrated within his concept of the 'dreamy state' (now known as mesial temporal epilepsy). In doing so, he described the current concept of elementary and complex auditory auras. Hughlings-Jackson also associated the auditory aura with seizures that began in the "primary auditory cortex."

Children with this type of sensory inward tuning do indeed almost seem to be in a 'dream state,' locked into a world from which they seemingly cannot be retrieved. Their concentration appears to be focussed upon something, which simply cannot be heard by anyone else, which of course is correct!

Tactile Problems

Quite simply, tactility is the sense of perceiving touch. If you were to be stroked gently, you would be receiving a gentle tactile experience. If a cat scratched you, you would be experiencing a harsh tactile experience. As with the other major areas of sensory experience, tactile reception can be disturbed by brain-injury. Children who experience difficulties with tactile perception, can display difficulties in their language, social and mobility development, in addition to experiencing problems with hand function as these areas all form the output parts of sensory – motor 'input – output loops.' The sense of touch is instrumental in communication and relationship building (language and social development.), whereas the implications for mobility and hand function of not being able to feel where your limbs are, is obvious.

The problem of ***wide spectrum tuning*** in tactile terms is a difficult one to identify, but some people suffering this have reported a situation where they are aware, in sensory terms of all parts of their body equally: - They are unable to focus on one sensory experience, on one area of skin, as all areas, which are in contact with the environment, are simultaneously active. The child has difficulty in filtering out sensations to which he does not need to pay attention. It seems that the neurological structures, which over-excite the cortex, are working overtime with the consequence that it seems there are so many parts of his body, which are passing sensory messages through to his brain that he cannot selectively attend to an individual tactile experience. It is as though the message gets lost in the melee of the sensory overload, which his processing system has to deal with.

Another distortion of tactile processing is that of ***narrow spectrum tuning.*** Children who experience this type of problem are only able to focus on one tactile stimulus at a time, so for instance, if you were to tickle their arm; they would be unaware of any other simultaneously occurring sensory experience. This can pose serious problems, as it can with children who suffer 'under-amplification' difficulties, because whilst focused upon a single sensory stimulus, they are unaware of any other sensory stimulus in the environment, even potentially dangerous ones.

Many psychological representations of such narrow spectrum tuning difficulties presuppose that tactile attentional systems operate to filter out extraneous information in order to shield our limited-capacity processing systems from information overkill (Posner and Cohen 1984). In the case of our child who suffers narrow spectrum tuning difficulties, the filter is acting too efficiently, - its spotlight is too focussed.

It has been recognised that in primates and debatably in humans, the neural chains for tactile processing are ordered serially, with the main synaptic projections going from the ***thalamus*** to the ***cortex.*** Yet again, it seems we have the thalamus heavily implicated in the sensory distortions, which our children face and we have evidence to support this. Experiments on monkeys have confirmed that the suggestion that a simpler structure in the brain, called the thalamus, contains a mental searchlight that filters what people pay attention to.

Kerry McAlonan and colleagues at the National Eye Institute in Bethesda, Maryland, say that this suggestion was made way back in 1984 by the co-discoverer of DNA Francis Crick.

The thalamus was once thought to be only a highway that connects the eyes to the brain's outermost layer and main site of consciousness, the cortex, which is responsible for housing the attention steering mechanisms that sort out all this sensory input.

During the course of the study, the researchers trained three macaque monkeys to pay attention to rectangular spots of light, each about the size of a thumb held up at arm's length. Their results show a quick surge of activity in the part of the thalamus that relays information to the cortex and, a split second later, a drop in activity in the thalamic reticular nucleus (TRN), a satellite structure known to turn off this superhighway of sensory information during sleep. The researchers think that when one pays attention, the TRN glances at the "images" coming through the thalamus and selectively turns on and off relays to pass on only the bits that deserve attention. (http://www.newscientist.com/article/dn14869-crick-was-right-about-vision-filter-in-the-brain.html)

Some children are under-sensitive in tactile terms and these are the ones who 'bump' into things seemingly without hurting themselves. These children are experiencing ***tactile under amplification.*** They can be covered in bruises and abrasions, which never seem to bother them. Many of them give the impression of being 'sensory – seeking missiles,' as they hurl themselves around. At the severe end of the scale, they are the children who can appear to 'self-abuse.' They may sometimes even go to the lengths of injuring themselves in order to try to feel some sensation. Parents have to take great care with children who suffer this difficulty as they may inadvertently cause themselves harm.

We have all seen or heard about children who can bite, scratch, cut and hurt themselves in multitude of ways and have thought, 'I wonder what makes them want to do that?' Well, have you ever considered what it may be like to have a sense of touch that is so dampened that you cannot really feel a great deal? You might begin to pinch yourself in order to feel some sensation. If that did not work, you might bite yourself in order to try to establish that there is some level of sensation. After many attempts at this and in utter frustration at still not being able to feel much sensation, you may become utterly frustrated and especially if you suffered other problems, which impeded your understanding, you may inadvertently begin to harm yourself, not understanding the implications of your actions.

This is the situation faced by many children who experience under-amplification difficulties. The sensory system's tuning mechanism is simply not exciting the cortex sufficiently to allow it to process environmental sensory stimuli adequately.

Children with this difficulty can sometimes seem aggressive, making excessive physical contact with other people and touching other children in too forceful a manner. This child seeks out tactile experience and may seem 'clingy' in wanting to be constantly held and cuddled.

At the opposite end of the scale, we see children who experience ***tactile over-amplification.*** Children who are over-sensitive in this area hate to be touched, they can sometimes pull themselves away from all contact. Tactile experiences, which you or I might take for granted, can send them into paroxysms of fear. They may be sensitive to specific types of sensation. One young girl who I know could not bear to have wool next to her skin, she would scream in apparent agony. It took her mother a while to discover what was causing the problem; - she removed the offending textile and the situation improved. I have also known a child who was over-sensitive down one side of his body and under-sensitive down the other side! These children evade making bodily contact with other people and objects in the environment, leading to poor sensory understanding and social remoteness. A child who is uneasy with touch may not feel secure and comforted by a parent's embrace; indeed he may avoid it like the plague.

The final distortion of tactile processing I wish to discuss is ***tactile internal tuning.*** The concept of 'internal tuning' is a difficult one to grasp. Have you ever suffered from what is known as 'pins and needles,' (paraesthesia)? At some time, most of us have experienced this phenomenon. It is a sensation of uncomfortable tingling or prickling, usually felt in the hands or feet. The affected area is sometimes said to have 'fallen asleep'. A common cause is leaning or lying awkwardly on a limb, which either presses against the nerves or reduces the blood supply to the local area. Changing position quickly restores normal feeling. Any numbness is soon replaced by the tingling and prickling sensation, as the nerves start sending messages again to the brain and spinal cord.

It is documented that in some cases, the 'pins and needles' phenomenon is caused by damage to the central nervous system. This state of affairs can be persistent and troublesome and can be caused by a large variety of sources, including brain-injury. This sensory activation can occur in any area of the body. Other types of paresthesias include feelings of cold, warmth, burning, itching, and skin crawling. Paresthesia occurs when an area of the body loses its normal sensation to touch. It may feel like a burning, pricking, tickling, or tingling sensation.

In some, but by no means all cases of brain-injury, this tactile phenomenon is a constant feature. The sensory system is creating its own 'interference,' which the tuning system is keying the cortex into, making it difficult if not impossible for the child to be aware of stimuli from outside his system; - from the outside world.

The development of the sense of touch not only helps to stimulate physical growth, it also plays an important part in emotional development. (Berk, 1997; Stepakoff, 2006). Could this be why children with the type of brain-injuries, which cause certain types of autism, are so emotionally distant?

The development of all 'output' abilities,' (language, fine motor development, mobility) are dependent upon and develop only after sensory abilities have developed. This leads us to a principle of treatment: - In any case of brain–injury / dysfunction, sensory assessment and the development of a programme to enhance sensory development is a first priority.

One point to note with children, who in sensory terms are 'over-sensitive,' whether it is visual, auditory or tactile over-sensitivity is the chaos, which can ensue for the child's sleeping pattern. I realise how important this subject is to many of you who simply do not sleep, because your child does not sleep. – I was in this situation for sixteen years as my own brain–injured son was one of the 'night-hawks.'

Mobility

Children with a wide variation of developmental disabilities experience problems with their motor development. Most people, even those who have little experience of children, are familiar with the major stages of mobility development. Most of us know that first, baby holds his head up, then later he rolls, sits up, crawls (first on his tummy, later on all fours), then he stands and finally walks. Many of us have seen this process; - those of us who have not, probably know the sequence. It is in the area of mobility that the difficulties caused by brain - injuries often become most obvious and most open to public scrutiny. We have all seen children in wheelchairs, children in standing frames, callipers, crutches etc. Lack of development in this area can be one of the first outward signs that many parents become aware of, regarding their children's difficulties.

As a cause of these problems, there could be many areas of the brain, which may have been injured, (a ***scattered*** injury), or there may be just one particular area of the brain, such as the motor cortex which may have been injured, (a ***localised*** injury). Depending upon the severity of the injury, the developmental pathway can be blocked in varying places. Some children with very severe injuries might never achieve any independent movement at all. Others with less severe injuries might make limited progress, whilst some with mild injuries might develop quite well.

Mobility might also be impaired by stiff muscle tone, indicating injury to the motor cortex, midbrain, brain stem, or corticospinal axons, depending upon the type of stiffness, or muscle tone might be loose or floppy, indicating injury, or lack of development of the cerebellum.

Another constraining factor upon the development of mobility occurs when a child retains the primitive postural reflexes. These reflexes, located in the hindbrain, are usually overlaid by more sophisticated movement patterns controlled by higher centres of the brain. Retention of these reflexes indicates lack of neurological development.

Language and Communication

It is ***the*** outstanding feat of the human brain that within eighteen months of birth, an uninjured human child, who has entered this world possessing no language, has an understanding of his native tongue and has begun to talk. That this leap into the use of symbolism is accomplished in what seems such an effortless manner makes it even more astounding.

The development of language and communicative abilities within a child with neuro-developmental problems is literally the most vitally important matter to be addressed and is the key to overcoming other problems faced by the child. You may ask why? You may think that your child has so many pressing problems, both concerning his health and concerning other aspects of his disabilities that surely, language development cannot be as important as I claim. In response, I would ask you to consider a child who possesses no language; in fact, he is unable to communicate at all. The fictional child we are discussing here, (although there are many non – fictional children such as this), suddenly develops a temperature and is obviously distressed. Ultimately, the doctor is called. The doctor arrives, surveys the visible symptoms, concludes that the child is suffering from a generalised viral infection, prescribes medication and leaves. Two days later the child is hospitalised. Unknown to the doctor, he was suffering from appendicitis, or he could have been suffering a kidney infection; - it could have been one of a hundred things, which through no fault of his own, the doctor missed, because the child was not able to indicate where he was hurting. – Communication is ***vitally important; - it can mean the difference between life and death.***

Also, consider the importance of communication and language to two other issues, ***motivation*** and ***understanding,*** and the role these two play in learning and development. A parent carrying out activities, which are designed to stimulate their child's development, is faced with two problems. Firstly, how do they motivate their child to want to do the things, which must be done? First we need to throw out the notion that children and their brain cells can be ***programmed*** in the way a computer can be programmed. – There is no evidence to support this notion. (There is a difference between 'programming' a brain and encouraging 'plasticity.' We can evidentially prove the plasticity of the brain, (it is called ***long term potentiation*** and conversely, ***long term depression),*** whilst there is no evidence that a brain can be programmed with sensory – motor, or any other type of information). We need to abandon the view that a brain can be programmed and try to encourage the view that children are equal partners in their development, - that a programme of developmental activities is carried out ***alongside them,*** as much as possible with their cooperation. Children cannot be 'programmed;' they are living, breathing, vibrant beings who have their own minds and who deserve respect for that fact. If I should use the word 'programme' within this text, it does not in any way denote the type of 'programming' to which I allude here, I am referring to a schedule of developmental activities, which provides the child's brain with the optimum opportunities for plasticity and development.

The motivation our children need to carry out developmental activities can only come through communication and through language: - If language and communication are not present, we must attempt to develop them through playful interaction. It is unusual for a child without even the slightest communicative abilities to be able to resist play for long, if it is presented at the correct intensity and level of ability.

My second point is that of ***understanding.*** Again, this relates to motivation. The more a child understands, the more effectively he can be motivated. In turn, the most effective way to increase understanding is through language and communication. This is an example of how learning leads development. If a child understands the need for him to carry out a task, which in turn will improve his developmental abilities, then the easier our task becomes. So let's take a look at the problems parents face with regard to their children's language development.

It is normal for parents not only to want their child to be able to understand them, but to be able to communicate with them too. Interaction is fundamental to humanity and in a way I feel it defines who and what we are. Naturally then, when a child cannot use language, it can cause parents immense distress. So why does the language and communication development of children with cerebral palsy and other neurodevelopmental problems so often fail? Let's examine some of the major reasons.

Many difficulties with the development of language and communication begin very early on, when the parents bring their child home after birth, or after the child has received the diagnosis. Naturally the parents are often weighed down by the worry and crippling stress of having to cope with their child's unexpected problems. I have been in this situation myself and can testify that it is so. Often they are reeling from the shock of the diagnosis their child has just received.

What frequently occurs then is that parents do not interact with their child as they would have done had they had an uninjured baby. They may miss the communicative signals given out by the child and consequently may not supply their child with input which is appropriate to the development of language. This is no fault of the parents, who are invariably doing an heroic job in simply caring for their child's needs and helping them survive despite sometimes overwhelming difficulties - This can often be a 48 hour per day task in itself! The situation is merely a result of a set of circumstances produced by the extremely stressful situation in which the parents find themselves.

So, having missed the early communicative opportunities provided by normal parent / child interactions, the child's early communicative skills fail to develop. Instead, the child sometimes completely fails to develop a communicative understanding with Mum and Dad, with the consequence that the understanding of language is impaired or even non-existent! In the absence of understanding of language, the child fails to produce language. In other cases where some appropriate but incomplete interaction has taken place between parents and child, a partial understanding of language develops, with little or no production of language.

A second reason for the failure of language to develop is when the child experiences 'distortions of sensory processing.' The brain abnormalities and dysfunctions which produce neurodevelopmental problems like cerebral palsy and autism, can adversely affect the functioning of several key structures in the brain, which are responsible for the processing of incoming sensory information from the environment. Obviously, we all know that successful development of spoken language is largely dependent upon successful auditory development; - Essentially, if the child's ability to process the sounds which make up the sound system of the English language is poor, - then their ability to reproduce those sounds as language will be poor. If their ability to process those sounds is non-existent, their development of spoken language is likely to be non-existent. It is simply a matter of successful sensory reception leading to successful motor output. (Language after all, is an output skill). In other words, this is a sensory - motor loop, the successful development of the motor part of the loop, being dependent upon the successful development of the sensory part of the loop. So, if we have a child who hears nothing, we are likely to have a 'NINO' situation, (nothing in - nothing out). If we have a child who is experiencing sensory distortions, whose hearing is hyposensitive or hypersensitive, or who is experiencing difficulties in regulating their auditory attention, we will probably be facing a CICO situation, (Chaos in - chaos out).

Other factors which can influence language development are difficulties with maintaining eye contact, reluctance to look at faces and the lack of ability to share attention with a communicating partner. These are all vital precursor skills to language development and form their own sensory - motor loops to support the development of communicative skills.

Another factor which will affect the development of spoken language is direct injury to the left hemisphere of the cortex, around the regions of Wernicke's area and Broca's area. These areas are respectively responsible for our ability to understand and produce spoken language. The connotations of direct injury here are obvious.

Another factor to consider is that when a child has a brain dysfunction or injury, the ability of their brain to process information is slowed down.

As a consequence they might not be able to process the content or meaning of interaction quickly enough and even if they can, they might be unable to respond quickly enough. The development of such conversational turn taking is a vital precursor to the development of spoken language. If the child keeps missing its turn in the interaction because his speed of processing information has been slowed, this can be very frustrating for the child who desperately wants to interact. This frustration at constant failure might lead them to simply stop trying!

The question is then, what can we do to assist the language development of our children? What I do at Snowdrop is to treat these causal factors logically and methodically.

First we need to take parents and their child back to the point where the interactive processes broke down. This can often mean going back to the beginning to the initial patterns of interaction, which have been missed. We need to teach parents to look for communicative signals given by their child and to foster meaning in the child's signals. Very often, these simple procedures can 'kick start' language development and we can then guide both parents and child through the next stages.

We also need to address any distortions of sensory processing which the child may be experiencing. This might mean the temporary construction of an adapted developmental environment in order to attempt to retrain parts of the brain which are responsible for sensory processing to re-tune their activity to a more normal level. - This is entirely possible and can often provide a massive boost to language development.

The next problem, which involves direct injury to the areas of the brain involved with language comprehension and production can be problematic, but depending upon the extent of the injury, is certainly not hopeless. The reason those areas of the brain are not functioning correctly is the fact that out of the millions of neural networks involved with these functions, many have lost cells due to injury. Therefore many networks are operating with their cell complement depleted. The effect of this is that they operate less efficiently and language comprehension and production are constrained. We can however use stimulatory techniques to train these networks to operate more efficiently, which encourages 'sprouting' (dendrites forming new synaptic connections, thereby increasing network efficiency). This neuroplasticity is the basis of recovery of function.

The final problem, relating to slower speed of processing, is perhaps most easily addressed. Quite simply, children must be given more time to process information, more time to plan a response and more time to execute that response. In this way they will not miss their turn and will not be tempted to withdraw from us in frustration at their perceived failure.

So whilst the difficulties faced by our children might seem great, indeed from my own experience, sometimes I know they seem insurmountable, - parents should not lose hope. If we can take children back through those vital early stages of language development, stages which they might have missed, then it is surprising what sometimes can be achieved.

Other problems of language and communication

There are many forms of language and communication difficulties, some of which can be misleading, leading the professional to conclude that the child's problems are not merely to do with language, but that they have a totally different problem, such as autism.

I was called into a small local primary school by the head teacher, who was convinced that a young girl in her class was on the autistic spectrum. The girl in question was reticent, socially isolated, keeping herself well away from others and her language and communication skills were severely retarded. It took three sessions of observation to draw the conclusion that this was definitely not autism! It turned out that the young lady in question was suffering an SLI, (specific language impairment). Her poor communication abilities were having such a dramatic effect upon her morale that she had simply retreated into herself and stopped trying to communicate. I suppose if you fail at something every time you try to do it, in the end you simply stop trying for fear of further failure. It took two years of patient painstaking teaching, taking the young lady back through the earlier stages of language development, through which she had failed to pass, to achieve a situation, where today she is a bright, happy, socially active young lady, who's social and academic prospects are now normal!

There are many other patterns of brain-injury, which can cause a myriad of difficulties with the development of language and communication. Children may experience these difficulties as 'stand-alone' problems, or they may experience them as just a part of a more complex set of issues, such as cerebral palsy or autism. Such difficulties include, speech production difficulties such as ***Broca's aphasia***, where the child produces sluggish, halting speech, or ***Anomia,*** which is characterised by word – finding difficulties. Then there is ***verbal apraxia***, where the child displays difficulties positioning speech sounds in the proper order.

A difficulty of speech production common to children with the pattern of brain-injury, which produces cerebral palsy, is ***dysarthria***: - a disorder in which the muscles, which are utilised during speech, are weak and badly coordinated. Consequently, speech is slower, imprecise, uncoordinated and slurred.

Some of our children also suffer speech comprehension difficulties, such as ***Wernicke's aphasia***. This is a set of difficulties where the child displays deficient speech comprehension and produces incoherent speech. It is caused by injury to the posterior part of the frontal lobe. Meanwhile, injury to part of the temporal lobe can cause a phenomenon known as ***pure word deafness.*** This condition reveals itself as the incapacity to understand the meaning of spoken words.

Yet another type of aphasia is ***transcortical aphasia***, of which there are three types; - mixed, sensory and motor. The child who experiences these difficulties has a tendency to repeat words to the point of sounding like an echo.

Children who suffer from ***conduction aphasia*** are not capable of repeating words spoken to them. Spoken language is comparatively steady, although the child might regularly correct himself and some words may be omitted or reiterated. Even though they are able to understand spoken language, it can be challenging for the child who suffers from conduction aphasia to locate the precise word to express their thoughts.

Another type of aphasia is ***paraphasia,*** which is characterised by the construction of inadvertent syllables, words, or phrases throughout a child's spoken discourse. Children with types of aphasia where spoken language is smooth display many more paraphasias than do those whose aphasia produces broken, halting speech.

Finally, for the major aphasias from which our children may suffer, there is ***anomic aphasia***. The child suffering from anomic aphasia has immense difficulty in recalling the names of familiar objects. For example, presented with a banana, he will say ***'oh yes, it's a, a, a, - yellow thing, you peel it and eat it.'*** They are not able to directly label it a banana! We have all experienced this phenomenon, where the name of something is just maddeningly out of our grasp. These children suffer the situation constantly.

Although many children with developmental disabilities will not attain literacy at all, some children who have milder injuries may become literate. It is therefore appropriate to quickly review the difficulties involved in literacy acquisition.

Problems of the written word.

Dyslexia

There are many forms of dyslexia, but here I shall concentrate upon the ones, which most commonly afflict children, they are ***surface dyslexia, phonological dyslexia and deep dyslexia.***

Surface dyslexia

This is a recent discovery. In 1973, Marshall and Newcombe described a pattern of reading disorder, which became known by this name. Approximately 75% of English words are what are described as ***regular*** words. The term 'regular' means that the particular word is spelled largely as it sounds. In other words, the word conforms to the rule that the sound of the word maps directly onto the way it is spelled. Examples of words, which obey this rule, are; 'dog' 'lamp' and 'scowl.' The remaining words of the English language, which make up the last 25% of English vocabulary, do not conform to these 'spelling to sound' rules and are known as ***irregular*** words, or ***exception*** words; These words have as a minimum, one infringement of the rule which states that the sound of the word should map directly onto the spelling. This can occur with a word like ***pint,*** which when presented to the child with surface dyslexia, will be read in the same way as the words ***hint*** and ***mint***.

The defining symptoms of surface dyslexia are:

- Irregular words are more often read incorrectly than are regular words.

- When an irregular word is not read correctly, the reading mistake is usually an error to do with regularisation. In other words, it is read as per the rules for mapping sound onto spelling. For instance, as I have just highlighted, ***pint*** is read as if it rhymed with ***mint.***

An explanation of surface dyslexia

There is a great deal of evidence that there are two pathways in the brain, which we use when we read a word; - one is the ***phonological*** pathway, which is the route we use when we read a word by sounding it out either out loud; or in our heads. We are literally building the word sound by sound. The second pathway is the ***visual*** pathway. - We use this when we read a word by ***sight recognition***, without the need to apply the phonological rules: - We simply recognise the word by sight! Because the phonological pathway reads words by applying spelling to sound rules, (in technical terms known as ***grapheme to phoneme correspondence***), it will miss-read words which do not conform to those rules; indeed, it will produce what are known as ***regularisation errors*** with these words. Hence- the word ***pint*** will have its sounds read by the phonological pathway in the same way as ***hint, mint, tint, stint,*** etc.

Consequently, according to this representation, accurate reading of irregular words is not dependent upon the phonological reading pathway but is dependent upon the ***sight recognition*** (or what is known; as the ***lexical***) pathway. Any injury to this pathway will have the consequence of producing what we now know as surface dyslexia. Non-words (That is, made up words such as ***stront,*** and ***magily,***) and normal, regular words will still be read accurately, but reading irregular words will have the consequence of producing regularisation errors.

Phonological dyslexia

Shallice and Warrington (1980) were amongst the first to identify phonological dyslexia, which can develop as a consequence of brain-injury or dysfunction. Children with phonological dyslexia demonstrate difficulties when reading ***nonwords*** (such as ***stromp,*** or ***retance***). These are words, which fulfil the rules of English phonology in that they are constructed as you would expect a word to be constructed; - however, they are not words within the English vocabulary. Some children who experience this problem also have difficulty in reading certain other types of words, such as function words.

The problem here, is that injury has taken place somewhere in the brain's ***phonological*** reading pathway. The child may still be able to read, because he learns to recognise words visually and can consequently use the ***sight recognition*** pathway, to read the words he knows. However, when it comes to reading a word, which is unfamiliar to him, such as a non-word, which we have invented, he simply cannot do it! He cannot do it because he has no access to the skills he would need to sound the word out, to literally build it sound – by – sound.

There are several theories as to what is going wrong in the brains of children who have dyslexia. The first has uncovered evidence via improved brain scan technology which has assisted researchers in uncovering some fascinating areas of research. For instance, groups of neurons which are found on the surface of the left and front brain (areas that are important in reading and writing), in people who do not have dyslexia have been discovered to be beneath the surface in people who do have dyslexia. It has been hypothesised that these cells failed to make the journey to the correct destination, which they should have when baby's brain was developing in the womb.

The second theory involves the brain's 'magno-cellular system.' This group of structures are a part of the brain which is involved in our ability to see moving images. Some studies have shown that this part of the brain may be smaller in people who have dyslexia, which in turn may lead to problems in the operation of decoding the images of words that the eyes see.

A third theory concerns which hemisphere of the brain children with dyslexia use when reading. When a child is beginning to learn to read, EEG activity is greater on the right side of the brain. In a proficient reader, there is more activity on the left side. In children with dyslexia, there are different variations in left-right activity.

A fourth theory involves the function of two structures in the lower brain, - the medulla oblongata and the cerebellum. Some researchers claim to have found differences in the structure and functioning of these brain structures in people who have dyslexia.

The truth probably is that any one, or indeed a combination of more than one of these explanations is a causative factor in different individuals. Oh, and similarly to autism, - don't forget that for some children there is a genetic explanation, - dyslexia can run in families!

Dysgraphia

Children, who are fortunate enough to have developed to a level where they may begin to attempt to encode language in writing, also suffer some peculiar problems. One of these is ***dysgraphia,*** and the consequences of these difficulties should not be underestimated. I have suffered from a form of dysgraphia all my life. This means that my handwriting is poor and badly sequenced, I place spurious letters in the middle of words; - in short, I do not seem to be able to sequence the thought processes needed in order to successfully transcribe the thoughts which are in my head onto a piece of paper. It is a completely different matter when I approach a keyboard, where I have no difficulty at all. Strange, isn't it?

Dysgraphia is caused by neurological difficulties, which express themselves by causing disordered and chaotic writing. Words may be varying sizes, be miss-spelled or sentences may even have words within them, which bear no relationship to the meaning of the sentence. The problem is thought to be caused by ***information processing*** difficulties.

Dyscalculia

Dyscalculia is a condition, which is not as well-known as some others. It basically means 'mathematics difficulty.' The causes of dyscalculia are not very clear, but there do seem to be difficulties in visual processing, which are associated with the condition. It seems as though the child simply does not 'see' mathematical situations, confusing numbers and making elementary mistakes. Another associated difficulty seems to involve 'sequencing,' which is an important ability when dealing with logical mathematical problems.

Dyspraxia

Although dyspraxia is a condition, which affects far more than language development, its effects upon speech and language are significant and consequently it is appropriate to discuss it here.

Children who suffer from dyspraxia can display immense difficulty in controlling the pitch and volume of their speech; they may also speak in a seemingly continuous manner, with their rate of speech also being badly affected. However, as I have inferred, dyspraxia can affect all areas of development, - and could prejudice a child's ability to learn. Typically, it is considered to be a disruption of the organisation of motor development. Nevertheless, connected to this might be problems of communication, awareness and cognition.

Difficulties occur in the progression of shaping ideas and in the planning and execution of movement. Children who suffer from dyspraxia suffer inferior comprehension of the signals, which their sensory systems convey to the cortex and problems relating those signals to actions. (Sounds like some of our other children with sensory distortion problems, doesn't it?). Therefore, physical actions are challenging to learn, tricky to maintain, and uncertain and inelegant in execution. Dyspraxia can affect each child differently and at different stages of development. How an individual is affected is inconsistent, too. For example, one day he may be able to perform a specific task, the next day he may not. This could be due to the day to day changes in the physiological environment in which the brain operates.

Signs and symptoms

Children who have dyspraxia might be behind schedule in reaching developmental landmarks and might display difficulty with simple physical tasks such as hopping and jumping, or balancing on one leg. They may have difficulty in coordinating their actions sufficiently in order to dress and may have immense difficulty walking on stairs or steps. Language and communication may be under-developed or incoherent in their early childhood and may develop at a slower rate than normal. In their school lives, children suffering from dyspraxia can experience obstacles with mathematics and writing, - especially writing in an organised narrative such as writing a story.

They may well evade games, display clumsiness when trying to dress and tying shoelaces will be especially problematic. Their overall level of organisation is likely to be poor and they could very well display problems with attention. They may possibly also experience difficulties with short term memory, consequently finding it difficult to follow instructions. Deficient handwriting is one of the most frequent symptoms.

Causes

Any injury to the brain may result in the individual experiencing dyspraxia. It could be caused by neurons, which didn't develop correctly at some stage in development, or oxygen deprivation during birth might be to blame. It may be a consequence of brain-injury brought about by infection, cerebrovascular accident or one of a hundred other causes.

Problems of Socialisation

The ability of the infant to co-operate in interacting with others is instrumental in developing a sense of self and of others as being separate from self and it is an ability, which is often lacking in children who suffer certain types of brain – injury. In particular one tends to think of children labelled as being on the autistic spectrum, in addition to children with Asperger's syndrome, Rett syndrome, children with corpus callosum dysfunctions, Angelman's syndrome to name but a few. Hence, we should review it here.

The drive toward co-operation with others seems to begin at an early age and as we have discussed, it is seen in the ***synchrony*** (cooperation*)* of early proto-conversations. The co-operative skills involved in the turn taking of proto-conversations are learned through early interaction with parents and lay the foundations for later language / conversational abilities. In itself, this turn taking routine marks some rudimentary sense of separateness from others. Indeed, research has shown that not only do babies engage with their social partners with mutual contingency from birth, but also, from as young as six weeks they are attempting to interact in a coordinated, co-operative fashion. (Trevarthen; 1995; Murray and Trevarthen, 1985).

Despite this early co-operative behaviour, some researchers still claim that infants have no sense of self in the early months. The position taken by these researchers comes from evidence gained from the ***'mirror–nose test'***, where it was only by the ages of fifteen to twenty - four months that infants in fact did reach for their own, 'rouge painted' nose, instead of their reflection, indicating their realisation that the reflection was themselves. (Lewis & Brooks – Gun, 1979).

However, there are many displays of co-operation by young infants, which indicate that the sense of self and other people may be more sophisticated than these researchers claim. Infants as young as six months have been known to produce ‘checking behaviour,’ co-coordinating their own view of a situation with their carer’s view of the same situation. This surely indicates a sense of self as being ‘apart’ from others? (In this instance, the carer). They will also engage in ‘play fighting’ and demonstrate fear of strangers. This indicates an awareness of being ‘apart’ from the person being play–fought and latterly, ‘apart’ and different to the stranger of whom they are wary. Unfortunately, the effects of a brain – injury / dysfunction can preclude the opportunity for the development of the sense of self and ‘other.’

A year old infant can adjust to take in the perspective of another person, in order to co-operatively share an experience; ‘perspective taking’ being a central tenet of many accounts of development. – Its necessity derives from social interaction, (which is itself a co-operative endeavour), which further promotes it. The interesting question is, whether this seeming drive towards co-operative social interaction is causal in promoting the development of a sense of self and sense of others. The evidence suggests that it is indeed the co-operation within these early interactions, which triggers the development of a sense of self and ‘other’ as being separate entities. Some children with brain – injuries tend not to be involved in such early co-operative interactions for two reasons.

(1). the nature of their difficulties prevents the child from interacting appropriately.

(2). Parents of children who have such difficulties tend not to interact with their children as parents interact with uninjured children. (This is not the fault of the parents, but a consequence of the immense stress, which naturally comes with adjusting to the child’s difficulties).

Therefore, we have a situation whereby the very means of development (normal interaction with parents) is denied to this group of children.

Research has shown that the sense of self / sense of other undergoes further development in the second year and that it is the child’s understanding of the emotional states of others, which precedes understanding in other areas, such as understanding the mental states of others. (Stern, 1985).

It is at this time the child begins to develop ***internal working models,*** of both themselves and others. (This is a mental representation of either oneself or other people. It comprises physical appearance and personality attributes). The types of models developed by the child are again linked to the word 'co-operation.' Secure (co-operative) attachment experiences and relationships tend to produce the development of positive internal working models whilst insecure (uncooperative) attachment experiences cause more negative models to be developed. Here again, the situation appears to be that 'co-operative' social experiences are moulding the sense of self and the sense of 'other.'

Unfortunately, due to the circumstances, which surround the child's problems, in some cases children who suffer brain injury do not have the opportunity to develop their co-operative skills and therefore do not form the secure attachments of which I speak.

This view is supported in many studies where it has been demonstrated that infants who experience secure (co-operative) attachments develop more self-awareness, more featural knowledge of themselves and others, higher self-esteem and better self-concept, than children who experience insecure attachments or who are maltreated. (Does not a neuro – developmental disability 'maltreat' a child?) (Pipp, Easterbrooks and Brown, 1993).

The development of language has a dramatic effect upon the child's ability to co-operate, both through discussion, which is a co-operative activity in its own right and through co-operative and pretend play. It is at this point that children are considered co-operative enough to become what Rogoff (1990) describes as ***apprentices in thinking.*** (This is a point in time where children develop their thinking abilities because of active participation in activities under the guidance of their caregivers).

Indeed, at this point children gain a fresh sense of self-awareness, brought forth by the advances the child makes, both in linguistic competence and production. This new sense of self is most evident with the child's use of self-descriptive terms such as 'I,' 'me' and the use of his own name. Again we see that a co-operative situation, facilitated this time by language, enables the child to make advances in self-awareness.

(Schaffer, 1996).

The importance of play.

When children play together, as they do in a more and more co-operative fashion after the age of three years, they are demonstrating a range of skills. During play, they are engaging in a highly co-operative way and demonstrating a sophisticated level of intersubjectivity. One of the most important venues for children to interact in this way is at preschool, which provides excellent opportunities for them to utilise and sharpen these skills by providing the opportunity for them to engage in co-operative and pretend play with their peers.

However, many children who suffer brain injury, even if they have by some miracle managed to develop this far in social terms, are not afforded the appropriate opportunity, or due to the severity of their problems are unable to engage in pre-school activity.

One of the features of play in children in their third year is the way in which their pretend play, which until now has been based within a role of compliancy, becomes more social and shared with other children. There is evidence that the nature of pretence in play is to allow the child to gain an understanding of his own emotional life. It has been demonstrated that children's representations during pretend play originate from significant emotional experiences in their lives. (Dunn, 1991).

The very act of pretence requires a sophisticated knowledge of both self and other people, because the child must demonstrate the capability of taking on the role of a pretend person who may have emotions and thoughts which may not coincide with his or her own. This clearly shows the child's growing ability to understand the mental states of others and is supported by other evidence, such as the fact that during the second half of the third year, children do begin to speak about their own and other people's mental states. (Dunn, 1991).

In addition, the level of intersubjectivity and ***metacommunication*** witnessed in pretend play scenarios requires colossal co-operation between playmates. (*Metacommunication is the negotiation of the direction of pretend play by two or more play partners. Also the negotiation concerning symbolic objects and their use, i.e., using a saucepan to represent a helmet*).

The co-operative play and pretend play fostered by the 'preschool' situation is of great benefit to children as they gain the opportunity to sharpen the skills, which will enable them to achieve a better understanding of themselves and others. To highlight this point it is interesting to consider the fortunes of children who have difficulty with co-operative and pretend play.

Children have a need to be able to understand the perspective of others in order to accurately predict their responses, in addition to guiding their own actions; - Many researchers call this ability ***theory of mind*** and it an ability, which is notably lacking in many children who suffer some types of brain – injury, notably on the autistic spectrum. (*Theory of mind is an understanding of the perspective and intentions of other people, used to predict what another person might do or say next).*

There is evidence to support the notion that children who are part of a larger family develop these abilities earlier than children from smaller families. It seems to be co-operative interactions with siblings, which facilitates the child's attention being focussed on the state of mind of his / her siblings. This enables the child to develop insight into their mental state. (Schaffer, 1996).

There is also evidence that the development of 'theory of mind' is dependent upon children engaging in pretend play. The question, which needs to be addressed is; - is the fact that so many children who suffer from brain - injury, do not engage in pretend play, the reason why they show a deficiency in the development of theory of mind? Obviously, there will inevitably be a large proportion of children whose severe physical and intellectual limitations automatically exclude them from participation in pretend play and this has a detrimental effect upon their development. - It is an interesting subject.

It has been suggested that the ability of children to understand the minds of others is influenced by interaction within the family. In a study of families in Cambridge, correlations were found between the frequency and extent of family interaction and the later ability of children to understand the minds of others. As I have already pointed out, children who suffer brain - injuries are often not afforded the opportunity to interact in this way, - or they are prevented from doing so by the severity of their problems. (Dunn, Brown & Beardsall, 1990).

Around the third year, further evidence for children's growing ability to understand the minds of others can be seen within family interactions. Consider the evidence from one family where a child in her third year had an older, only sister who possessed imaginary friends. In order to upset her sister, the child would transform her own identity and claim the identity of one of the imaginary friends! This shows an understanding not only of herself as a separate entity, but also of the attributes of the imaginary friend. It also demonstrates a great deal of determination and imagination to infuriate her older sister! (Dunn, 1991).

It follows that further co-operative interaction, facilitated by siblings and peers in family and preschool environment, particularly the opportunity afforded for the child to participate in co-operative and pretend play, further augments the child's growing knowledge of self and other people. We somehow have to facilitate this in the children we seek to help.

Sleep

As the father of a child who for sixteen years, hardly ever slept, I have experienced the mind numbing tiredness and anxiety this situation produces. I have also witnessed its effect upon my child and other children and families in similar situations. The daily stress of taking care of a child with brain-injuries is compounded because of lack of sleep. So what is sleep and why is it so important to us?

There is an argument as to whether sleep is an altered state of consciousness or a behaviour. – The argument is academic and irrelevant if you are being deprived of it! The assertion that it is a behaviour may appear a little bizarre, because we usually visualise a behaviour as something, which entails movement. However, apart from the rapid eye movements, which are associated with a particular stage, sleep is not characterised by movement. Because we recall very little about our sleep, apart from the occasional dream, most people have a tendency to view sleep more as an 'altered state of consciousness.'

There are several structures in the brain, which are important for the regulation of sleep; they are the ***hypothalamus, suprachiasmatic nuclei, reticular activating formation and pons.***

Most people are aware that there are different stages of sleep and will at least have heard sleep broken into two categories, ***REM sleep*** and ***non – REM sleep***. There are actually five stages of sleep, incorporating REM sleep and four stages of non REM sleep. Let's take a look at the most well-known phase of sleep first, REM sleep. During REM sleep, we dream and the eyes move rapidly, (hence the term, REM – rapid eye movement). This type of sleep occurs for a few minutes at approximately 90 - minute intervals during the night, which means that throughout a typical night, we dream several times. The rest of the time, we are travelling through the other, non-REM stages, with stage 4 sleep being the deepest level. During REM sleep, our body musculature is disconnected from the neural centres, which control it. This happens for our own safety, so that we do not 'act out' our dreams. In fact, physiological studies have shown that a person actually becomes paralysed during REM sleep. (Carlson. 2007).

The ninety - minute period seems to be important not only for sleep, but in general terms, as it appears to transfer to our everyday activities. It was Kleitman (1961), observing babies who were fed on demand, who first noticed a ninety - minute cycle appearing. Later studies discovered ninety - minute periods of rest and activity in adults too, for such activities as eating, drinking, stomach motility, and ability to pay attention. (Kleitman, 1982).

These findings are significant when we consider our children. In uninjured children, it is the demands of the social environment, which suppress this ninety - minute clock. The pattern of life in the Western industrialised countries means that we need to work all day and sleep all night. – This pattern forces us and our children to override the internal clock and our children, within a relatively short space of time of being born, are usually sleeping through the night. In some non - industrialised countries, in Africa for example, there are tribes whose parents carry their children around with them whilst they carry out their daily activities. As far as sleeping is concerned, these children and parents have a tendency to fall into the ninety-minute pattern during day and night.

When a child has suffered brain-injury, he may not have the sophisticated level of neurological organisation to override this ninety - minute cycle and to comply with our pattern of life. Therefore, from our point of view, his sleeping pattern is chaotic and disturbed, as is his pattern of activity during the day. In point of fact, his sleeping pattern may be naturally conforming to this body clock and may be perfectly normal; - it is our pattern of activity which is wrong!

It seems we do not need to sleep in order to overcome the trials of our physical workload during the day. There have been studies of sleep deprivation with human subjects where it has been conclusively proven that sleep is not needed to keep the body functioning normally. (Horne,

1978). However, if we are deprived of sleep, it does seem to affect our cognitive abilities, so it seems that sleep is primarily needed by the brain, not the body.

So, apart from the ninety – minute biological rhythm, to which many of our children appear to be naturally complying, - why do so many of our children experience sleeping difficulties? There are many other reasons.

There are many sleeping problems our children can display depending upon the nature and extent of their brain-injuries. ***Sleep apnoea*** is a problem for many adults, but it can also be a problem for brain-injured children. Sleep apnoea is where the person stops breathing during sleep. The brain then causes the person to wake suddenly and breathing restarts. They literally have difficulty in sleeping and breathing simultaneously. Macey et al (2002) have highlighted that this problem can occur because of early brain damage and the way in which the developing, injured brain 'wires itself.' It can also be caused by a build-up of carbon dioxide in the bloodstream during sleep and the child (or adult) wakes gasping for air (Carlson, 2007). The poor development of the breathing pattern of children with brain-injuries can only exacerbate this situation. Fortunately, it is only a small minority of parents who report this problem with their children.

Another problem, which concerns sleeping, is ***narcolepsy***, which is caused by the brain's inability to adequately regulate wake / sleep cycles. In this condition, the child will suddenly fall asleep, regardless of what is happening around him. The 'sleeping attack' will last only a few minutes and he will wake again. This problem seems to emanate in a part of the brain called the ***hypothalamus*** and involves a failure in the processing of a special class of neurotransmitters called ***hypocretins.***

Neurotransmitters are special chemicals, which brain cells produce to communicate with each other and to regulate biological processes. The neurons which produce hypocretins are active during wakefulness, and research suggests that they keep the brain systems needed for wakefulness from shutting down unexpectedly, which is exactly what does occur in narcolepsy.

Related to narcolepsy is ***cataplexy***, which involves a sudden loss of muscle tone, so that the person abruptly falls to the floor. This can easily be mistaken for a type of epileptic activity known as ***clonic*** seizures. As I have discussed, one of the primary features of REM sleep is muscle paralysis, - a disconnection of the muscles from the control centres in the brain. In cataplexy, this disconnection from neurological control occurs at unusual and unpredictable times and the child simply collapses.

There are two further categories of sleeping difficulty to which, due to their brain-injuries, our children can be assigned. – Firstly, there are children who ***cannot sleep***; - these children have to push themselves to a state of exhaustion before they sleep and can stay awake for days. I once knew a child who managed to solidly stay awake, and to consequently keep his family awake for eleven days and nights! His poor parents were exhausted!

Secondly there are children who can sleep, but ***do not do so at the correct time.*** Their sleeping pattern (circadian rhythm) is not operating correctly. These children may be conforming to our ninety-minute cycle or may be affected by some other neurological system malfunction.

Looking at the first category of children, those who cannot sleep, their difficulties may have various causes. First, we need to consider that the cause may be sensory in nature. It is very difficult for children who have sensory over-amplification difficulties to sleep. The slightest noise, such as a creaking floorboard, visual stimulus such as a mobile in the room, or tactile stimulus such as the sheets rubbing against the skin, will be sufficient to guarantee lack of sleep for the child who suffers from this type of sensory difficulty. As I have hinted, children with this type of problem will sometimes stay awake for days, sleeping only when pushed beyond the point of exhaustion.

What can be done to improve their prospects for sleep? Well, children who visually over-amplify should have a bedroom, which is free of visual clutter. The room should be as dark as possible with all mobiles and posters removed; in short, the room needs a dampened visual environment.

The child who suffers from auditory over-amplification difficulties is a different kettle of fish however. It would be difficult to supply an auditory environment, which was absolutely quiet. This child hears the slightest noise, a floorboard creaking, the tap running in the kitchen; he is so sensitive he almost hears you think! - This child hears *everything* no matter where it is in the house, no matter how quiet you think it is. The only thing to do is to mask the noises, which keep him awake. This can be done by keeping a constant gentle background noise in his room. As I previously discussed, it is best not to use CD's or tape recorders, which are likely to click when the CD or tape has finished; - the most effective way is to leave a radio on in his room all night, just at a gentle background level. This should be enough to provide a mask for any other noise, which may occur.

The child, who over-amplifies in tactile terms, hates bedtime. The rubbing of sheets against the skin, the cool air of the bedroom; - all guarantee a level of over-stimulation, which serves to guarantee lack of sleep. The first priority with this child is to keep the bedroom warm enough so that you do not have to cover the child with sheets or a quilt. Ensure the environment is free of anything, which may accidentally come into contact with the child. This may improve the situation.

The second cause of sleeping problems involves the brain in other ways. Sleeping patterns are influenced by the patterns of light and dark around us. Light hits the retina and this message is passed to a set of brain cells called the ***suprachiasmatic nuclei.*** The suprachiasmatic centre is one of the body's major biological clocks. It not only regulates hormones related to the day/night cycle and therefore our sleeping cycle, but also orchestrates the activities of many other internal clocks. In numerous experiments, it has been shown that, when the SCN is not innervated, the human body clocks free-run; they set their own time. It has also been shown in studies of sleep disturbance that among the visually impaired there is a higher incidence of sleep impairment. Due to these visual impairments, the suprachiasmatic cells are not receiving enough stimulation from light in the environment. (Are not many of our children visually impaired to some degree? This would certainly apply particularly to children who suffer visual under-amplification difficulties).

We now have reasons why many of our children have chaotic sleep patterns, the question is; - how can we address this?

The sleep cycle can be influenced in many ways. Firstly, many of our children, because of their physical disabilities do not get the same amount of exercise as their well compatriots. Moderate amounts of exercise have been shown positively to enhance the sleep pattern. A programme of visual stimulation at the correct time of day can also stimulate the suprachiasmatic nuclei into influencing the sleep / wake cycle, as can simply allowing our children to sit in sunlight at the right time of day. There are also dietary methods, which can positively influence sleep. The right foods, at the right time of day, can help to positively influence sleep; - For instance, a small amount of banana, which contains ***tryptophan***, a few hours before bedtime, can help the onset of sleep. (Tryptophan is a precursor of the neurotransmitter 'serotonin,' which we need to produce in order to bring on sleep).

If all these techniques fail, as they sometimes do, you could consult your doctor concerning a prescription of 'melatonin' a naturally occurring hormone, which promotes sleep, whose production in the brain is stimulated by a reduction in the amount of light in the evening. (***You must consult your child's doctor before administering any medication to your child***).

As an absolute last resort, in the most severe cases, your doctor can advise you on the use of more powerful medications, which may ensure a night's sleep. Beware though, these medications, such as chloral hydrate, or benzodiazepines are very strong and addictive. They can also promote side effects and 'hangover' effects.

Ultimately, sleep may always be a problem. I have encountered many children who have taken enough medication at night to knock out an elephant and still they have stayed awake!

The Effect of Sleep upon Learning.

Sleep is very important to both learning and memory formation, - which is a vital component of learning. It is almost as though our brains are practicing what they have learned during the day, whilst we are asleep! - Even when we are dreaming.

Ever heard the adage ' if you have a problem, sleep on it?' Well it is not just an old wives tale because there is evidence that sleep enable subconscious learning processes to kick into gear and to reinforce what needs to be encoded in memory.

In one experiment two groups of people were taught new typing skills. The first group were denied sleep that night, whilst the second group were allowed a full night's sleep. The group who were denied sleep had forgotten almost everything they were taught the previous day, whilst the sleep group performed much better.

Another study involving new-born babies demonstrated that Even though infants may stay awake for just a few hours a day, their brains keep working around the clock. It seems that the brain is constantly adjusting and adapting to the physical world despite appearances that babies are sleeping.

Tests on one and two day-old babies showed that their ability to act as "data sponges" – absorbing information about the world around them – never stops. The discovery was made by researchers at the University of Florida after simple experiments with 26 sleeping new-borns. Researchers played a tune to them, and then followed it with a gentle puff of air to the babies' eyelids. After about 20 minutes, 24 of them had learned to anticipate the puff by squeezing their eyes shut. The babies' brain waves also changed.

Dana Byrd, a psychologist, said, "We found a basic form of learning in sleeping new-borns, a type of learning that may not be seen in sleeping adults. "They are better learners, better 'data sponges' than we knew. While past studies find this type of learning can occur in infants who are awake, this is the first study to document it in their most frequent state, while they are asleep.

"New-born infants' sleep patterns are quite different to those of older children or adults in that they show more active sleep where heart and breathing rates are very changeable.

"It may be this sleep state is more amenable to experiencing the world in a way that facilitates learning."

The results, published in the journal Proceedings of the National Academy of

Sciences, could be used to identify babies that are not developing properly such as those at risk of dyslexia or autism, she added.

Again, we see a principle of treatment arising from this research. It is that intensive, day – long programmes do not give our brain – injured babies sufficient 'down-time' to be enable them to employ their subconscious learning processes and to encode into memory the information which is provided within their programme of developmental stimulation. A programme should be flexible and non – intensive and should give plenty of periods of rest!

Why the past has failed. - Physiotherapy

When a child is diagnosed as having a brain - injury, the diagnosing doctor very frequently, automatically refers that child to a physiotherapist. This seems the logical and natural course of action; - the child might after all, have problems with muscle tone and with his joints. But is it the correct course of action? We will review the evidence to discover the truth!

In the UK, as in most other European countries, physiotherapy is based upon one of two systems of treatment, - the Bobath method (sometimes known as 'neurodevelopment therapy), or the Vojta method. The most common method and one which was employed upon my son for a short time was the Bobath method. Let us briefly summarise the theoretical underpinnings of each system, before moving on to assess their effectiveness.

The basic goals of Bobath physiotherapy are: -

1. The prevention of postural deformity

2. The stimulation of normal developmental processes through the facilitation of normal patterns of movement.

These goals are operationalised by utilising several principles.
The first principle involves the inhibition of abnormal reflex patterns in the child. According to Bobath, as the child grows older and his central nervous system matures, the activity within the system falls into well-worn patterns.

A good example of this can apparently be seen in the child with a stiff muscle tone. The pattern of activity, with which the brain responds to any external stimulation, has the effect of further increasing the child's muscle tone. It is claimed that this occurs because, due to the child's brain injuries, there will only be a limited number of synaptic chains (chains of communicating brain cells) available to register a response. (Bobath, 1980. P. 79)

The techniques used by the proponents of Bobath therapy, apparently serve to inhibit these abnormal motor responses, (the stiff muscle tone), by handling the child in such a way as to prevent the muscles from becoming stiff. In inhibiting these abnormal patterns of movement, the opportunity is apparently created for more normal movement patterns to occur, which are the remit of higher levels of the brain, and which have been prevented from occurring by the stiffness of the child's muscles. (Bobath, 1980. p. 79).

The principle which underlies this theory is as follows. - It is the body musculature, which determines the state of the central nervous system. It is the body musculature which controls the opening and closing of connections within the central nervous system and determines the subsequent outflow." (Bobath, 1980, p. 83).

Does the musculature really exert influence and control over the state of the central nervous system? Surely this cannot be the case? Has the cart not been placed before the horse here? Surely it is the brain which controls the status of the body musculature?

Bobath cites as evidence for this view, the experiments of Van Uxwell, who studied the response to stimulation of primitive organisms such as Starfish. Briefly stated, he concluded that the "results of any stimulation can be predicted by looking at the body musculature." (In Bobath, 1980. p. 83).

Bobath appears to be drawing a false interpretation from Van Uxwell's experiments by implying that stimulation is directly affecting the status of the body musculature, which in turn is influencing the activity within the central nervous system. Such an interpretation does seem to be the wrong way around. Surely what is actually happening is that stimulation of the muscles is being transmitted into the brain by afferent, (inbound) nerve fibres; - the stimulus is then registered and interpreted within the brain and it is the brain which organises a response from the muscles via it's efferent, (outgoing) nerve pathways.

Although the state of the musculature reflects the pattern of activity within the central nervous system, to state on the basis of this evidence that it is the musculature which is influencing the brain is clearly a mistake!

The second major principle underpinning this approach involves the stimulation of higher mechanisms of control in the child. Such mechanisms comprise 'righting reactions' and 'equilibrium reactions.' (Bobath, 1980. p. 8). These two sets of reactions are highly integrated and automatic responses to changes in posture or movement, aimed to restore disturbed balance.

The problem here is that children who suffer brain injury, especially children whose muscle tone is stiff, (spasticity), invariably have suffered considerable injury to the cortex. Equilibrium reactions in particular require cortical contribution. (Bobath, 1980. p. 8).

As for righting reactions, which are organised at the level of the thalamus, again a considerable percentage of children who suffer brain injury have thalamic injuries.

So, the relevance of the implementation of a programme of Bobath physiotherapy for the treatment of brain injury must be called into question.

It is now appropriate to quickly describe the other major physiotherapeutic approach used in many countries, known as 'Vojta' physiotherapy. In the Vojta system, normal patterns of movement, for example, reaching and grasping, standing and walking, are not explicitly taught as such. Vojta therapy rather claims to arouse the brain, triggering 'intrinsic, stored movement patterns' which can then be "exported" as synchronized movements linking the musculature of the body and extremities.

It is claimed that frequent activation of these reflex-like movements, produces new 'networking' within the functionally blocked network of nerves between the brain and the spinal cord. For Vojta therapy to be successful, it is claimed it must be carried out several times a day. A treatment lasts between 5-20 minutes.

However, there may be dangers in the use of this type of physiotherapy. During forced active rotation and head retraction, one child suffered from bleeding into the adventitia of both her vertebral arteries, which prompted ischemia of the caudal brainstem with subarachnoid haemorrhage. One wonders if comparable cases have arisen, but have not been registered. There may be a delay involving the performance of physiotherapy and the beginning of such neurological indicators. (Jacobi G, et al, 2001).

Is there any evidence for the effectiveness of any physiotherapeutic approach, regardless from which school of thought it may derive? The answer has to be that down the decades, there have been various studies, although most of them poorly designed, most of which have indicated that children who have brain injuries do not benefit developmentally from physiotherapy.

In one of the earliest studies on record, children suffering from cerebral palsy were divided into three groups as follows: -
Children who received physiotherapy for twelve months.
Children who received no physiotherapy for six months, followed by six months of physiotherapy.
Children who received no physiotherapy at all.

At the end of the study, no significant differences were found between treated and untreated children in any of the criteria under observation. The concluding remarks were telling!
"It is felt that advice on the skilled handling of the severely handicapped child, initially in a therapy situation, imparts confidence to the child and the parents and that this is perhaps the major contribution of therapy." (Wright & Nicholson, 1973).

The second major study in the seventies also produced discouraging indications for the efficacy of physiotherapy. Twenty four children under the age of eighteen months, with an initial diagnosis of cerebral palsy were divided into two groups, an experimental group and a control group. The experimental group of children received physiotherapy for six months, whilst the control group received no therapy at all. At the end of the six month period it was found that there were very little differences between the groups, with the children who had been exposed to less physiotherapy showing slightly better results. For the more severely handicapped children, there was no difference at all. (Sherzer et al, 1976).

So, as early as the mid 1970's the evidence pointed to the lack of success of physiotherapy as a treatment tool for brain injury. We now move to the 1980's, where a further two studies shed light upon the approach. In the first study, 48 infants, with moderate to severe spastic diplegia, aged between twelve and nineteen months of age were randomly assigned to one of two groups. The first group received twelve months of physiotherapy. The second group however received a six month period of infant stimulation, (consisting of sensory, cognitive and language stimulation), followed by only six months of physiotherapy.

Assessment was performed after both 6 and 12 months of therapy to evaluate motor quotient, motor ability, and mental quotient. It was found that the children who had received the stimulation programme and less physiotherapy performed better on all measurements. - Another nail in the coffin of the physiotherapist as developmentalist. (Palmer, 1988).

The other major study in the 1980's was a review of all previous studies and was severely critical of the methodologies employed by all of them. However it too concluded that; *"Evidence for the usefulness of this therapy has yet to be demonstrated."* (Tirosh et al, 1989).

We now move to the year 2000 and to a study in which 55 children with mild or moderate cerebral palsy were assigned to two groups, one a group which received physiotherapy and one which did not. The children were tested on a range of measures at six, twelve and eighteen months. At the end of this time the researchers found no difference between the two groups in any of the functional skills under scrutiny. (Ketelaar, M. et al. 2001).

A clear picture is emerging is it not?

In the last forty years, despite all of the research which has been carried out, only one study demonstrates any meaningful improvement in brain injured children who underwent a regime of physiotherapy and that single study was carried out by an employee of the Bobath centre, - a major provider of physiotherapy! The lack of independence of this study calls its validity into doubt and this will undoubtedly be pointed out by some of the researcher's peers. So to re-summarise, there are no truly 'independent' controlled studies which support the use of physiotherapy.

Despite the evidence, the medical profession continue to tout physiotherapy as a developmental tool, with which to treat brain injured children. The evidence states that this is definitely not the case. The knowledge to help brain injured children is out there, as I will demonstrate to you, - it is simply not utilised!

Having set aside physiotherapy as a useful approach to stimulate development, allow me to summarise why it does not work.

The focus of physiotherapy, despite what its proponents might claim, is upon the symptoms of brain injury. Those symptoms include the muscle tone of the child, whether stiff or floppy, scoliosis, fixed deformities, tremors etc. Never is any attention paid to the cause of those problems, - the injured brain.

Allow me to highlight this attitude by recalling a conversation I had with a paediatric physiotherapist. She stated that my son had very severe physical problems (symptom). I responded by confirming that yes, his brain - injuries were very serious. Her response to this was to say, “Yes, his brain injuries are bad, but he also has terrible physical problems.” She could not see that the physical difficulties my son faced were caused by his brain - injuries and that were the brain - injuries not present, neither would be the physical problems, because one was a symptom and the other was the cause of that symptom.

Please do not misinterpret what I am saying. I am not saying that symptoms have to be ignored. Indeed it could be dangerous to ignore some symptoms, such as epilepsy! Yes, symptoms need to be controlled, but they should not be treated in isolation. If we are to succeed in treating brain - injury then we also have to develop cause centred approaches. Physiotherapy is not one of them, - we can prove it is not one of them and it would behove health professionals well, to stop touting physiotherapy as a developmental solution to brain - injury. In doing so, they are misleading parents in just the same way as they accuse alternative treatments of doing so!

You will note that I am careful in my use of words concerning physiotherapy. - I denounce its use as a *developmental tool.* I do not deny its usefulness in other areas, indeed when utilised properly, physiotherapy is vital! The role of the physiotherapist in helping to prevent contractures and postural deformities is of exceptional importance. If the physiotherapy can maintain the integrity of the child's physical structure, then the developmentalist has a good platform to work from.

Why the past has failed. - Patterning

Patterning is a treatment rationale utilised by various clinics across the globe, with many variations in its application. It is a methodology which has come in for a great deal of criticism from many authorities and is judged to be one of the more 'controversial' therapeutic approaches, - so let's examine this desperately 'controversial' approach to treatment.

There are many organisations applying many variations of the patterning treatment, so much so, that it is impossible to attribute all theoretical standpoints to one particular organisation; - Some adhere to some theories, whilst others denounce the same theories. Necessarily then, this is a generalised review.

One theoretical standpoint is the *'recapitulationist'theory.'* Some patterning organisations hold the belief that 'ontogeny' recapitulates 'phylogeny.' - All this means is that they hold to the idea that the development of a child from conception to maturity is a replay of the evolutionary development of our species. Of course it is absolute nonsense and allow me to demonstrate why?

The theory says that at any point in his development the movement patterns of the human child will replicate the movement patterns of species which are lower down the evolutionary ladder.

This seems an attractive theory and on the surface it does appear to have some truth in it. After all, does a new-born baby not wriggle like a fish? Does a seven month old child not adopt the same movement when crawling as an amphibian? Does a child who is crawling on his hands and knees not adopt the same movement pattern as a reptile? When a child first starts to walk, does he not hold his arms up in the air like an ape? The answer is yes, to all these questions. However, some of the proponents of patterning go further than to note these resemblances and attribute participation of definite levels of the brain to these developments. - This is where the theory falls apart!

According to recapitulation theory, the following logic applies.

1. They claim that because the dominant level of the brain operating in a fish is its medulla, and the fish produces wriggling movements, this means that the dominant level of the brain in a new-born baby, which produces similar wriggling movements, must be the medulla!

2. Because the dominant level of the brain operating in an amphibian is the pons and the amphibian produces 'homolateral' movement patterns (moving the arm and leg on the same side of the body simultaneously), this means that the dominant level of the brain of a young child who produces these patterns of movement must be the Pons!

3. Because the dominant level of the brain operating in reptiles is the midbrain and the reptile produces a movement pattern called the 'cross-pattern,' then the young child producing the same pattern of movement, must be operating at the level of the midbrain.

You get where I am going with this?

What seems to be forgotten in this simplistic view of development is that although yes, we do share the same brain structures as species lower in the evolutionary scale, in human beings the functions of those structures have been transformed! According to some proponents of patterning then, because the human cortex developed from the olfactory bulb, human beings must think by smelling! It is patent absolute simplistic nonsense!

The second major belief of many patterning organisations is that of *'individual sequential development.'* Put simply, this is the belief that the brain develops in definable stages, from bottom to top and that the brain stage above cannot begin its development prior to the completed development of the stage below. In this view, beginning from the bottom of the brainstem and working upwards, the first brain structure to develop is the 'medulla oblongata.' The next stage above the medulla, the 'pons' cannot begin its development until the medulla has completed its development. The stage above the pons, the 'midbrain,' cannot begin its development until the pons has completed its development. - This apparently continues all the way up to the cortex, which according to some patterning theorists is the final stage of the brain to develop!

This of course is absolute nonsense! We know and can prove that the cerebral cortex exerts a controlling influence even in a new-born baby!

The next claim of some of the patterning organisations is that the brain is under-used; - that we only utilise a small percentage (the claim is usually 10%) of the total capacity of the brain. The proposed implications of this proposed under - use are that even a child who is profoundly brain - injured will possess sufficient spare brain capacity to make recovery of function a viable possibility.

Let's nail this myth!

The idea that we only use 10% of our brains is probably such an enduring myth because it's comforting to think we have spare capacity. The 'unused' 90% could take up the slack after brain - injury or offer the possibility for miraculous self-improvement. This flexible factoid has been used not only to sell products to enhance our brain's performance, but also by psychics and their supporters to explain mystical cutlery bending powers!

Unfortunately the boring, tedious, but unavoidable facts point to this merely being a desirable myth and unfortunately there are four good reasons it's almost certainly false (Beyerstein, 1999).

1. If we only use 10% of our brain then damage to some parts of our brains should have no effect on us. As any neurologist will tell you, this is patently not true.

2. From an evolutionary perspective it is highly unlikely we developed a resource-guzzling organ, of which we only use 10%.

3. Brain imaging such as CAT, PET and fMRI shows that even while asleep there aren't any areas of our brain that completely 'switch off'.

4. Parts of the body that aren't used soon shrivel and die. Same goes

for the brain.

5. Any neurons we weren't using would soon shrivel and die as the brain pruned unused connections.

The structure of the brain and its metabolic processes have also been carefully examined, along with the diseases that afflict it. None of this work has suggested there is a hidden 90% that we're not using, – Unfortunately!

Anyone who still maintains we only use 10% of our brains after this fusillade of fact has to come up with a counter-argument for each one of these points. I see no valid argument to refute these facts!

Evidence for the use of patterning.

There is no available independent, controlled, peer reviewed evidence to support the use of patterning.

I feel on the basis of the evidence, that the approach to the treatment of brain - injury known as 'patterning' can be viewed as being based upon several false premises and an overly simplistic view of brain function and child development.

Why the past has failed. - Conductive Education

Conductive Education made its big splash in the UK in the 1980's. I remember seeing children from the UK boarding planes for Budapest to visit the Peto Institute. I also remember one TV interview with a father of one of these children where he called the Peto Institute a 'miracle factory.' Well, what is conductive education and how effective is it in treating children with brain - injuries?

Conductive education was founded by Dr Andras Peto and is described as a system for overcoming motor disorder. The goal of the system appears to be the creation of 'orthofunction.' Quite simply, orthofunction is the ability to function independently in the world despite one's underlying disability. (Sutton, 1989).

The proponents of conductive education (CE) therefore by definition are not promoting a cure. They are promoting function despite the disability, although Hari (1988), the leader of the Peto Institute speaks of "restoring children to health." - This seems at odds with the concept of orthofunction.

The major principle which underpins CE is that it is an educational approach; it encourages the child to develop through learning. This is a philosophy with which I totally agree and which has a great deal of evidence to support it. However, it seems that the acknowledgement that learning can lead development has an effect upon which children are suitable candidates for selection to receive CE. Children who have no understanding of language, or whose developmental disabilities leave them unable to interact with others, would be judged to be not suitable candidates. Children with severe visual problems, autism and epilepsy would also not be suitable candidates. (Sutton, 1989. Todd, 1990)

So, conductive education is not a form of therapy or treatment, rather it is a system of teaching and learning. It consists of several principles, a well-known one of which is the 'task series.'

A task series is a more complex learning objective, which has been broken down into several simpler sub-tasks, which can be learned one at a time until the more complex objective is completed. The way in which this is achieved is that tasks are apparently, 'taught, learned, practised, generalised and used.' This seems to borrow from the theories of a Russian psychologist, Lev Vygotsky, who asserted that the way in which children learn is to firstly require the assistance of others, (teaching and learning), when assistance of others is no longer required, the task can be executed independently and then over time, becomes automatic (practice leading to generalisation).

This is an excellent principle for teaching children with both learning and physical difficulties. If the information or task to be learned can be presented at a level, which is accessible to the child, then we make learning possible in even the most severely involved children.

Another principle of conductive education is that of rhythmic / verbal intention. This is again taken from Vygotsky's research at the turn of the twentieth century examining the relationship between inner speech and the development of literacy.

In Vygotsky's observation of young children he noticed that younger than the age of six or seven, children have a tendency to talk to themselves quite a bit. He noticed that even when playing side by side, they would sometimes prefer talking to themselves rather than communicating with each other. Upon closer examination of these self-directed conversations, he noticed that the children were actually giving a running commentary on the activities they were involved in. He called this running commentary a ***'personal monologue.'*** He noticed that what was in fact happening was that the children were thinking out loud. They were using this ***verbal thought*** to monitor, guide and control the activity in which they were involved. He also discovered that by age seven, this verbal thought had disappeared or been 'internalised' to become ***'inner speech'*** and that this was an important factor in the child developing the ability to read and write. (As you are reading this page can you not hear your own inner speech?).

Conductive education takes this outward verbal thought and uses it as a tool to help children to monitor, guide and control developmental tasks and to master tasks, which are essential for daily living and independent function. The only change they make, and I believe it to be a fatal one, is that they teach the children to sing, not talk. Now singing and musical ability are controlled by entirely different areas of the brain than talking! They call this singing 'rhythmic intention.'

Again, this is an excellent, if distorted use of a proven developmental process. The only differences I would have with the proponents of conductive education is that whereas they tend to focus upon teaching children tasks, which are essential for daily living, I believe its usefulness could be widened to incorporate teaching children with learning difficulties and it could be focused on more areas of development than it is currently.

The final major concept used within conductive education is that of the group. Group dynamics are harnessed and utilised to motivate the children towards achieving the goals which have been set by the conductor (the instructor who trains each group). In this 'learning group' the children not only learn from the conductor, but also from their peers. The advantages of working in a group like this can be seen from the plethora of research which has been carried out on group dynamics. Adherence to group norms and the power of social facilitation can be powerful factors in improving the performance of the individual.
So what does the research say about the success or failure of conductive education in improving the performance of children who suffer developmental difficulties? Well there has been a surprisingly small amount of research carried out on conductive education. I review three of the more prominent studies here, which demonstrate mixed results.

In the first study, 34 children with a diagnosis of cerebral palsy, matched by age, motor impairment and cognitive ability were randomly assigned to one of two groups. The first group undertook a programme of conductive education, whilst the second group undertook an 'equivalent intensity' control programme. It was discovered that children in the conductive education group made similar progress to the children in the more traditional programmes.

In the second study, results also suggested that programmes based upon conductive education are no more effective than other more traditional forms of intervention for children with physical disabilities.

In the third study however, where the objective was to measure developmental gains made by a group of children with cerebral palsy, who were on a programme of conductive education, compared to a similar group of children undergoing conventional community based therapy. The results in this study were more favourable. Skill gains by children with spastic quadriplegia, cerebral palsy and severe developmental delay who were not able to sit independently, who participated in the conductive education programme were significantly greater than skill gains by children with similar disabilities who participated in conventional community based therapy. Children in the conductive education group who suffered with quadriplegic cerebral palsy, severe developmental delay, epilepsy and sensory disabilities also achieved significant gains in functional skills. (Reddihough et al, 1998. Liberty, 2004. Bochner et al, 1999).

Although a great deal more research is needed, it seems that we have at least some indication that elements of conductive education could be a useful tool to incorporate into the treatment of brain injured children.

The criticism I would have towards the proponents of conductive education and it is perhaps a reason why only one of the studies I found highlighted any favourable results, is that it seems to be a miss-application of one of Vygotsky's theories and it is only utilised with a narrow range of children.

As I have already indicated, for a child to be a candidate for conductive education, he / she must have some grasp of language. Many brain injured children have tremendous difficulties in the area of language and communication development, which precludes them as candidates.

As for the apparent miss-application of one of Vygotsky's theories, Vygotsky believed that inner speech exercised a vital controlling function, not only in the development of literacy, but in many learning tasks. (Is this not so? - In learning a difficult task, don't we all 'talk ourselves through it?'). As I have already stated, in conductive education, the process of rhythmic intention is a deviation of the process of a 'personal monologue.' Instead of talking through the process of a task, children sing or chant their way through it. This is not inner speech as it is commonly used and this might possibly have affected its successful use.

These three approaches are the major therapeutic approaches which have been used to treat neuro-developmental problems in children over the past sixty years. In my opinion they have not succeeded and the evidence seems to support my view.

Why the past has failed: - Behavioural therapies

Various behavioural therapies have sprung up since the 1960's; I like to think of them as 'Skinner's offspring.' (B. F. Skinner is the father of behaviourism). Put in straightforward terms he believed that the behaviour of a human being could be changed by the use of reward and punishment, - indeed that behaviour could be shaped in the same way, so that undesirable behaviours were eliminated and desirable behaviours reinforced. Indeed, we have already discussed such 'conditioning' of children earlier in this book and the limited effect this approach can have.

A whole branch of psychology rose in the 1960's almost seeming to bear the fruit of the seeds which Skinner planted with a 'positivist' ideology which seemed set to change the world. - It didn't and it can't because human beings are not machines.

According to behaviourist principles, human beings operate on 'stimulus – response' principles. The person is subjected to a positive stimulus and the way he is currently behaving is reinforced, if he is subjected to a negative stimulus, his current behaviour fades and is ultimately extinguished. It is true that behaviour can be influenced in this way to a limited effect, but my question is, is it really solving the problem?

Consider a brain – injured child who has hearing which is very over-sensitive, as many of our children who have autism do. He is so disturbed by his hearing that every time he is exposed to some sounds he screams in agony. Behaviourist therapies would apply negative reinforcement and might well be able to stop the child screaming by doing so. This makes life much more comfortable for the parents and makes life generally more tolerable, but has it solved the child's problem? The child is still in agonies every time he hears the noise, but he has now been conditioned not to react by screaming, but to react in a different way! So we have changed the way the child behaves, but we have not changed the child's experience! He still suffers from over – sensitive hearing. I would question whether we, as parents would simply want to make life easier for ourselves whilst leaving our children in continuing agony.

ABA (applied behaviour analysis) is currently touted as an effective treatment for autism, but is this really true. It might well be an effective treatment for the behaviour which autism produces, but does it actually touch the cause of that behaviour, the autism itself?

The thing that really upsets me about some behavioural programmes is their use of 'aversives.' We have discussed the fact that behavioural approaches seek to eliminate undesirable behaviours by negative reinforcement (punishment), well some do so by the use of what are known as 'aversives.' (aversives are unpleasant stimuli, which induce changes in behaviour through punishment. The theory is that by applying an aversive immediately following behaviour, the likelihood of the behaviour occurring in the future is reduced).

The question is what aversives are used? Well there seems to be a range of them which are reported by parents. These range from therapists delivering a simple 'no' to a child, through to feeding children tobasco sauce when they produce undesirable behaviour and it is reported that there is one 'educational' centre which requires residents with autism to wear backpacks in which they carry a device which delivers a moderate shock to their arms or legs. The device is activated when they misbehave. http://autism.about.com/b/2007/12/26/aversive-therapy-for-autism-a-tool-for-good-or-evil.htm how horrific is that?!

Not all behavioural approaches use such extreme measures, but they mostly all use some form of negative reinforcement. Personally I would never use a form of therapy which subjected a child to any type of punishment, even if it was just verbal.

A New Beginning

So, let's begin at the beginning. Is the brain truly treatable? How do we get the brain to respond to treatment? How does all this information apply to children with brain injuries?

The answer to the first question is yes! Twenty five years ago the idea that the brain produced new cells throughout its life, (a phenomenon we call 'neurogenesis'), or that the brain was so plastic that it could alter its connections, effectively changing its structure and functioning was scoffed at by the medical profession.

Neuroscience has moved forward substantially in the past 25 years. An illustration of discovery and development over this time is seen in our construct of brain plasticity. Brain plasticity refers to the brain's ability to rewire itself, switching functions from one area of the brain to another, utilising different neural networks. 25 years ago, the belief was held that brain networks were static after the period of their initial establishment. That belief has now quite rightly been assigned to the dustbin of history and research into brain plasticity has profound implications for the treatment of children with neuro-developmental disabilities like cerebral palsy and autism.

In order to better grasp this concept of plasticity, we need to take a quick tour of the human brain and neural networks within.

The brain is a multi-layered structure in which billions of brain cells are connected together. They exchange information through grouping together to form neural networks. In the brain, each neuron is connected to up to ten thousand other neurons through synapses (specialised junctions where brain cells communicate with each other). A neuron receives input from other neurons through these synaptic junctions.

This is the basis of brain cell communication. It is also the premise for the formation of neural networks. These networks are formed early in life and are responsible for specific tasks, such as learning, pattern recognition, memory, etc. It was believed that once neural networks were formed, they would remain static and inflexible. However, research in the past two decades has indicated that this is not the reality: our neural networks are in fact flexible and responsive to change.

So what does it really mean to have a plastic brain? It has many implications to human developmental and learning and it illustrates the brain's ability to adapt to change throughout an individual's lifetime.

Let's look at this plasticity and apply it to children who have neuro-developmental problems like cerebral palsy in the following way. Children who have neuro-developmental disabilities have millions and millions of neural networks whose functioning has been disrupted by either the adoption of an improper pattern of connectivity, or the loss of brain cells. Unfortunately there is no 'quick fix' for this situation influencing brain plasticity takes time, - it is not an overnight phenomena, it is more of a 'slow drift' towards an intended goal!

For instance, in a few weeks of working with the child for a few hours per day, we might see some minor improvements. In a few months of working those hard long hours, some more substantial improvements might be seen, (or not, because children respond at differing rates depending upon the location and severity of any injury to or dysfunction of the brain). In a few years of working those long hard hours, some major improvements might be seen. Unfortunately there is no quick fix. Overcoming brain injury is a long, hard slog, of dull routine, of going over the same exercises and developmental activities again and again and yes, - again! This is how brain plasticity is driven.

Brain plasticity or neuroplasticity is the ability of the brain to build new connections, - literally to re-wire itself in order to allow the individual to function adequately in his or her environment. As we have just alluded, it is driven and guided by the environment, - it responds to the needs of the individual. We see this every day in ourselves, who fortunately are not brain injured. Look at this example. I recently learned to juggle, - it took me quite a while and many, many attempts before I managed to even begin to be able to do it semi - competently. As I was practising over these many months, very slowly my brain began to respond to the environmental demand I was placing on it and began to devote neurological resources to assist me in my task. It began to build neural networks which would enable me, bit by bit to master the function to which I was exposing myself. Eventually, with sufficient practice and with sufficient neural wiring built to support my activity, I became able to juggle. That is how brain plasticity works!

So, let's extrapolate this knowledge about plasticity to our brain injured children who are at home doing their Snowdrop programmes. For a start, the brain injury, - or the brain dysfunction if you prefer to call it that, creates a 'roadblock' in the brain, which slows down or stops everything. It slows down, stops or distorts development because it slows down, stops or distorts the brains ability to interact and take sensory information from the environment; - In doing so it impedes plasticity! What the Snowdrop programme is designed to do is to provide sufficient impetus through providing appropriate developmental activities in an appropriately enriched sensory environment. In this way we can increase or decrease the stimulation to which a child is exposed in order to accommodate the problems created by the brain injury. In this way we can overcome that roadblock and to get the traffic moving again.

This is why the repetitions of the activities within the programme are so vitally important.

In the same way that the repetitions of my juggling attempts were important to building plasticity, so are the repetitions of the activities within the programme! First we create the environmental demand through the activities of the programme and then we have to wait for the brain to respond. It takes time and patience.

Fortunately, with very young children we also have an additional ally alongside the plasticity of the brain and that is the fact that the brain of a youngster is growing fast! A baby's brain has the capacity to grow at an exponential rate. At birth, it is only one quarter of its adult size, but by three years of age, it will be 80% the size of an adult brain. At birth, it is one of the only organs that have not yet fully developed and it is sensory stimulation, received from environmental experience, which is the crucial factor in the development and efficiency of neural networks and optimum brain function.

So, you might say that the are two types of plasticity in the brain, the more rapid plasticity fuelled by the growing, interconnecting brain and the 'slow drift' plasticity which remains after the initial period of exponential brain growth has passed.

Another good example of this 'slow drift' plasticity comes from research carried out by Dr Hugo Spiers at University College London.

Magnetic scanners were used to explore the brain activity of taxi drivers as they navigated their way through a virtual simulation of London's streets, researchers said. Different brain regions were activated as they considered route options, spotted familiar landmarks or thought about their customers.

Taxi drivers have a larger hippocampus - a region of the brain that plays an important role in navigation, according to previous studies. Researchers said their brains even "grow on the job" as they build up detailed information needed to find their way around London's labyrinth of streets - information famously referred to as "The Knowledge".

Dr. Spiers said they were keen to go beyond brain structure - and see what activity is going on inside the brains of taxi drivers while they are doing their job. Functional magnetic resonance imaging (fMRI) was used to obtain "minute by minute" brain images from 20 taxi drivers as they delivered customers to destinations on "virtual jobs". The scientists adapted the Playstation2 game "Getaway" to bring the streets of London into the scanner.

The drivers were then shown a replay of their performance and reported what they had been thinking at each stage.

"We tried to peel out the common thoughts that taxi drivers tend to have as they drive through the city, and then tie them down to a particular time and place," said Spiers.

The scans showed a complex choreography of brain activity as the taxi drivers responded to different scenarios. The researchers said the hippocampus was only active when the taxi drivers initially planned their route, or if they had to completely change their destination during the course of the journey. Activity was noted in a different brain region when the drivers came across an unexpected situation - for example, a blocked-off junction. A separate part of the brain helped taxi drivers to track how close they were to the endpoint of their journey; like a metal detector, its activity increased when they were closer to their goal. Changes were also noted in brain regions that are important in social behaviour.

Spiers acknowledged that taxi driving is not just about navigation: "Drivers do obsess occasionally about what their customers are thinking," he said

Animals use a number of different mechanisms to navigate - the Sun's polarized light rays, the Earth's magnetic fields and the position of the stars. He said this research provides new information about the specific roles of areas within the brains of expert human navigators.

What this research does show is how the brain slowly builds the 'neural architecture' to enable individuals to function within the environment in which they find themselves. This is the essence of 'slow drift' brain plasticity and it is the essence of a Snowdrop programme of rehabilitation. In the same way that exposure to driving London's streets, encourages plasticity within the brains of taxi drivers, a Snowdrop programme, which exposes the child to demands for specific developmental functions, encourages and directs brain plasticity to build the neural architecture to support those developmental functions.

Very occasionally I will receive a call from a parent a few weeks after starting their programme saying, "nothing's happening, his spasticity is just as bad, or his epilepsy hasn't improved at all, or he isn't talking yet" - Well, things won't improve that quickly because this is not an overnight phenomena it takes hard work and patience. I take their calls with the same large pinch of salt as the parent who calls me after two days and tells me how much better their child is doing. The enthusiasm is nice, but it is the long term product to which I am looking. When I devise a programme I am looking months and years down the line at where I eventually want the child to be.

There is also the occasional parent who will tell me that she or he has tried my programme for a few weeks, (the shortest amount of time I had was one week) and that they were convinced that it wasn't going to work and that they were now going off to raise several thousand pounds for another miracle cure or quick fix. I just accept it because who says I wouldn't do the same? In fact I have done so! Thankfully, the overwhelming majority of my amazing parents knuckle down to work, realising that they can't cure this overnight and they need to work with their child for more than 20 minutes a day if they are to have any chance of having even a small effect, let alone rescuing their child! They are the people who produce miracles.

Learning and plasticity.

Let's also look at the way in which children learn and examine how learning is also a major beneficiary of brain plasticity. Studies with musicians and athletes have shown that particular areas of the brain responsible for 'fine' or 'specific' movements in certain parts of the body (e.g. the hands of a pianist or string musician) are in fact rewired for optimal efficient performance. Once training becomes a routine, and particular movements are repeated over and over again, the tendency is that neuronal connections will become more permanent. This is a useful finding for children who have brain - injuries as a repetitive programme of developmental stimulation can be designed with the aim of taking advantage of this plasticity.

Further recent evidence comes from research carried out by scientists in Tübingen, who have proven for the first time that widely-distributed networks of nerves in the brain can fundamentally reorganise as required.

Scientists at the *Max Planck Institute for Biological Cybernetics* in Tübingen have succeeded in demonstrating that the activities of large parts of the brain can be altered in the long term. The breakthrough was achieved through the experimental stimulation of nerve cells in the hippocampus, - a part of the brain known to be involved in memory and learning. Using a combination of functional magnetic resonance tomography, micro stimulation and electrophysiology, the scientists were able to trace how large populations of nerve cells in the forebrain reorganise. This area of the brain is active when we remember something or orient ourselves spatially. The insights gained here represent the first experimental proof that large parts of the brain change when learning processes take place. (Current Biology, March 10, 2009).

Like the cortex, the hippocampus consists of millions of nerve cells that are linked via synapses. The nerve cells communicate with each other through so-called "action potentials": electrical impulses that are sent from the transmitter cells to the recipient cells. If these action potentials become more frequent, faster or better coordinated, the signal transmission between the cells may be strengthened, resulting in a process called long-term potentiation (LTP), whereby the transmission of the signal is strengthened permanently. The mechanism behind this process is seen as the basis of learning.

Although the effects of long-term potentiation within the hippocampus have long been known, up to now it was unclear how synaptic changes in this structure can influence the activities of entire neuronal networks outside the hippocampus, for example cortical networks. The scientists working with Nikos Logothetis, Director at the Max Planck Institute for Biological Cybernetics, have researched this phenomenon systematically for the first time. What is special about their study is the way in which it combines different methods: while the MRI scanner provides images of the blood flow in the brain and, therefore, an indirect measure of the activity of large neuronal networks, electrodes in the brain measure the action potentials directly, and therefore the strength of the nerve conduction. It emerged from the experiments that the reinforcement of the stimulation transmission generated in this way was maintained following experimental stimulation. "We succeeded in demonstrating long-term reorganisation in nerve networks based on altered activity in the synapses," explains Dr. Santiago Canals. The changes were reflected in better communication between the brain hemispheres and the strengthening of networks in the limbic system and cortex.

Let's look at some real children where this inherent plasticity has been harnessed and utilised to speed their development. These are not fictional children with theoretical problems, but real live children with real problems. All of the children I am about to tell you of have been carrying out a Snowdrop programme for over a year. Some of them have made incredible progress; others have made some progress, whilst a few have only achieved modest progress.

Aaron.

When I first saw Aaron, he was eight months old. He had a twin brother and the difference between them was startling. Shortly after his birth, doctors had discovered that Aaron had a tumour at the back of his brain near the fourth ventricle. This caused hydrocephaly and matters were further complicated when part of the drainage device used to relieve the pressure on Aaron's brain had become infected and Aaron developed meningitis. When I first saw him, he was a completely passive and withdrawn little boy who had suffered serious brain damage. He had severe sensory problems, being almost completely unable to see, his hearing was variable and his sense of tactile perception fluctuated. His doctors had detected significant 'grey matter' damage. (The grey matter includes regions of the brain involved in muscle control, sensory perceptions, such as seeing and hearing, memory, emotions and speech). Aaron was therefore expected to have significant problems in all these areas.

I immediately instituted a programme of developmental stimulation which was to be carried out for two hours per day, five days per week, which was based upon Aaron's developmental needs in all areas. Mum and Dad carried out this programme religiously and the results have been nothing short of startling, - it seems we have disturbed a hornet's nest!

I see Aaron for the last time in a few months, (October 10) and he is a very different little boy. His Mum called me last week to tell me he had just walked across the room, was talking so much she couldn't keep him quiet and he was constantly competing with his twin brother, (and winning!) in every area. In comparison with his twin he is now equal, or maybe slightly ahead in every developmental area, so they have decided they do not need to see me anymore. They have worked tremendously hard and deserve credit for doing nothing short of saving their little boy. A happy ending! My final programme for Aaron will include a reading programme, so that by the time he goes to school, he will be well ahead of his peers intellectually.

Thomas.

Thomas is a five year old little boy who has a major structural problem in his brain; - He does not have a corpus callosum. The actual diagnosis is 'agenesis of the corpus callosum.' The corpus callosum is a collection of over 200 million nerve fibres which connect the left and right hemispheres of the brain. The effect of not having one is dramatic! Imagine the two hemispheres of the brain to be like two islands and the corpus callosum is a big, wide bridge, which connects them. This bridge is capable of carrying a great many people from one island to the other simultaneously, just as the corpus callosum carries a great many messages between the hemispheres, so that they communicate and act in harmony. If the bridge were not there then communication between the two islands would stop. In cases where children suffer this brain abnormality, the two halves of the brain are unable to communicate and as each half of the brain controls the limbs on the other half of the body, this lack of communication has profound effects.

Thomas shows many symptoms, which are typical of children who are on the autistic spectrum; - distortions of sensory perception, repetitive, compulsive behaviour, what seems almost an addiction to vestibular stimulation, he has no language and does not like to interact with people. To his parent's consternation he emits a constant droning sound.

When I first saw Thomas it was obvious to me that the droning was being used by him as a tool and it quickly became apparent what it was. Thomas found sound to be very threatening. Not a sound in particular, but ***all*** sound! He used the droning to drown out environmental noise so that he could not hear it. He replaced that noise, with his own, more comfortable droning noise, of which he was in complete control. Thomas has now been on programme for just a year and the droning has not stopped, but it is vastly reduced. He is tolerating more interaction with his environment and the people in it and has started to communicate with his parents. Thomas's Mum and Dad know that I am only ever going to have limited success with him because he actually has an entire structure within his brain missing and no amount of therapy can replace that. What I can try to do however is make the neurology which is present work to its maximum efficiency.

Michael.

Michael is a seven year old little boy from New York, who is on the 'distance programme.' In close communication with his parents and doctors and having seen DVD recordings of Michael's performance I was able to gain a good understanding of his developmental problems. Michael had a mixture of mild cerebral palsy and autism. He did not interact with people, but preferred to interact with objects. He had no language, was socially isolated and showed no imagination in his play. He did have some mobility and used this to walk round and round the table in his lounge to the point where it drove his parents crazy.- He had a favourite toy, - a train, which he played with to the point of obsession, being fascinated with the wheels, which he spun round manically and held very close to his eyes. He could not bear to be around other children, displaying extreme fear when placed in such an environment. Fifteen months later he is starting to use words for the first time and he uses them to interact with people, not objects.

His fear of children turned out to be a tactile problem, - a fear of physical contact, which is much improved. His lack of interaction with people was caused because he had missed out on those stages of development which were vital precursors for language development. Once I had designed a programme which encouraged him to retrace his steps and to complete these early developmental stages, his ability and willingness to communicate progressed very nicely.

Toby.

Toby is a ten year old young man who has moderate cerebral palsy, mixed with a good dose of ADHD. When I first saw him he never stopped, - he was one of those children who you find swinging from the chandelier one minute and then trying to jump out of the window the next. He was and is also a bundle of fun and has a great sense of humour. Toby was running his parents ragged, they looked close to exhausted, with a good side dish of frustration and bewilderment thrown in for good measure. I instituted a strict nutritional programme, mixed with a programme high in specific vestibular exercises for Toby, knowing exactly which neurochemical systems I wanted to influence and combined this with some techniques to build attention and concentration. Toby has been on programme for just under a year and he is a different child. The hyperactivity is not gone, but it is reduced. His teachers report that he is much more easy to manage in the classroom and actually carry out parts of his programme at school, which is great! Most of all, Toby is now able to stay still for long enough to communicate and his language development has flourished. He still has a long way to go, as do most of the children I see, but they are taking great strides!

Ross.

Ross is a four year old little boy from South Africa. His official diagnosis is cerebral palsy, but that does not do justice to the severity of his injuries. Ross is totally dependent in every way, for every aspect of his care. He is one of the children who literally don't know where their next breath is coming from. When I was first introduced to Ross, he could do nothing. I don't even think he was aware that his legs, arms and hands were there, let alone what they were for. He could not see and his hearing was over-sensitive to the point of being bizarre. I knew that with the severity of his injuries, progress was going to be difficult and maybe limited and so did his mum and dad, but together we set about a plan to attack his problems in a logical, methodical way.

I instituted a programme of sensory stimulation combined with the creation of an adapted environment to accommodate his auditory problems. I combined this with activities designed to promote mobility. The results were startling for Ross, who within nine months of being on programme was not only able to see sufficiently to begin interacting with his parents, but could also now use his hands to take of his socks and throw them!

At the other end of the spectrum, I should also mention the children who despite my best efforts do not make this kind of startling progress. Some make more modest gains whilst a few, frustratingly for the child, parents and me, make no progress at all. I do not know why this is, but a possible explanation comes to mind from a friend who happens to be a neuro-anatomist. His thoughts are that as we only understand approximately 60% of what goes on in the brain that this accounts for my failures. When we understand totally, we will understand why what we are doing is making no impact and be able to alter it!

I suppose we could say that these case studies of children which I have just presented demonstrate 'plasticity in action.' There are many more case studies I could cite, but I would quickly run out of space to write anything else.

But my child has learning difficulties!

Learning difficulties are another symptom of brain – injury. Your child's cognitive development has been slowed or stopped in the same way and for the same reasons that his other developmental processes have been slowed or stopped.

How the brain learns. – Plasticity in action.

In order to learn, we first have to perceive; - In order to perceive, whether by vision, hearing, touch, taste or smell, our sensory systems have to be functioning correctly. Therefore, learning is subservient to perception, which in turn is subservient to development of the sensory system. Consequently, the first goal in any learning programme with a child who has brain-injuries is normalisation of the sensory channels. We have previously discussed this.

As we have proven, when we learn, our brain responds to new information and as such, it must necessarily adapt its functioning. It achieves this through ***synaptic plasticity***, - the forming of new connections in the brain, or the strengthening of existing ones. Yang & Maunsell, (2004), in their work with primates were clearly able to demonstrate that learning involved changes in synaptic connections in the cortex, which established new neural connections. Again, we are back to the concept of ***neural networks***, - groups of brain cells operating together as a network to encode (learn) new information. In order to represent one piece of learned information, the network will connect together in a specific pattern, and in order to represent another piece of learned information, the same network might slightly alter its pattern of connections. This is the way in which brains learn and remember. – A memory being merely a representational pattern of connections!

There are many types of learning of which human beings are capable, which will create such connective networks in the brain. The simplest of these is ***conditioning***, of which there are two types, ***classical*** and ***operant***.

Classical conditioning is the style of learning made notorious by Pavlov's research with dogs. The general idea of the research was this: Pavlov offered food to dogs, and calculated their salivary reaction (how much they drooled). He then began sounding a bell immediately prior to offering the food. Initially, the dogs did not start to salivate until the food was offered, however, after a short time they began salivating when they heard the sound of the bell. They had learned to connect the sound of the bell with the offering of the food. In as much as their immediate physiological reactions were concerned, the ringing of the bell corresponded to the offering of the food; - It had become a ***conditioned stimulus.***

Classical conditioning however, due to its haphazard nature is difficult to use as a teaching method with children, our only reason for introducing it is to move on to another form of basic cause and effect, associative learning, that of ***operant conditioning.***

Whereas classical conditioning forms an association between two stimuli, (the bell and the food), operant conditioning forms an association between behaviour and a reward, (or punishment). The reward ***reinforces*** the desired behaviour. – In this way we are able to ***shape*** (encourage), desired behaviours with a reward and to eliminate undesirable behaviours with negative reinforcement. It is basic cause and effect learning, As I have previously said, I prefer not to use behavioural approaches such as this as I do not think to punish a child in order to 'teach' it is a desirable strategy; - I merely point to the fact that such a strategy exists.

With severely brain-injured children, a reward for the performance of a desired behaviour would need to be instantaneous, - or plainly linked to the behaviour. However, with children who understand some spoken language, we can make clear the relationship between the reward and the behaviour, even if they are removed in time. For instance, you might tell a child that you will give him a treat because he helped you to do something. With children who possess no understanding of spoken language, the relationship between the reward and the behaviour cannot be made explicit in this way. For these children, the reward has to be instantaneous.

As I say, this type of associative learning is the very first, simplistic step on the ladder to success. As I say, I do not like to use these behavioural approaches with children as I feel that changing the cause of the behaviour is better than changing the symptom, - the behaviour itself.

Fortunately, most brain-injured children are in advance of this level of learning and can be approached with more sophisticated techniques. Most children who suffer from brain-injury invariably have some type and degree of learning difficulty. These difficulties vary in their nature from individual to individual; - they also vary in severity. I differentiate between children in what I term ***organic learning difficulty*** or ***environmental learning difficulty***.

- ***Organic learning difficulties.*** *These are caused directly by the brain-injury, by direct damage to the cognitive structures of the brain, which cannot then operate correctly.*
- ***Environmental learning difficulties.*** *This is where the cognitive structures may be intact, but the brain-injury is preventing learning from taking place because it is causing sensory difficulties, or other problems, which prevent the child from interacting with the environment.*

Of course, some children ***appear*** to have greater learning difficulties than is actually the case, simply because their brain-injuries prevent them expressing the intelligence they do possess.

Many of the problems our children display as far as learning difficulties are concerned, involves ***speed of processing*** information. The brain is an information-processing machine, where networks of brain cells all happily and speedily communicate with one another. What then happens when suddenly one brain cell in the network is lost through injury? The remaining network of cells may still be able to process information, but without the full complement of cells in the network, the task is more arduous and therefore much slower. In time and with practice and proper stimulation, the network may become more efficient; - it may even be able to improve its performance by recruiting an additional cell to the network in order to restore the full complement. Now apply this scene to millions of networks in the brain, which are affected by oxygen starvation and which consequently lose cells and thus lose operational efficiency. Can you see how the whole process of learning and development can be slowed down?

Other major problems our children face are with memory and attention, which are vital functions needed to support learning; - if we cannot pay attention to information then our chances of learning are remote because we simply will not have access to the information which should have been learned and therefore will be unable to pass that information to memory. If memory is affected then we cannot remember all the information which has been presented to us. This obviously impairs the ability to learn!

Many people think abilities such as memory and attention are built into us from birth, but this is not the case at all; - they are learned! It seems the brain centre instrumental in supporting these abilities is a structure in the ***limbic system*** known as the ***hippocampus***.

We learn to develop our attention as young babies through the early interactions with our parents; developing what is termed 'intersubjectivity' and we can stimulate the development of those attentional skills in brain-injured children by taking them back through those early interactive episodes.

In a similar vein, we also learn memory functions. This is useful, because logic dictates that if we learn how to do something then by definition we must be able to find a way in which it can be ***taught.***

Consider when you are attempting to commit an unfamiliar telephone number to memory; what strategy do you learn to employ in order to achieve this? The solution is to keep repeating the number until it is ingrained in memory. By 'rehearsing' the number verbally, aloud in this way, you are constantly refreshing it in auditory memory. (Auditory memory usually fades after about one and a half seconds). This gives the networks of brain cells the extra time they need to process the information and to embed the information within the network, (to memorise it). This is just one simple technique by which our children's memory systems can be developed. For children who experience difficulties in the area of language, whilst we are working on developing those language and communicative abilities, it may be necessary for us to externalise techniques such as rehearsal by simply doing it for them; - by repeatedly presenting the information to be memorised and learned. There are also many games, which can be used to help develop these abilities.

In order for us to combat the learning difficulties which are faced by our children, it is important for us to understand how children learn. One of the great names of child development is Jean Piaget. He proposed that children's development proceeds in 'stages.' According to Piaget, a child cannot complete developmental tasks, which are in his next, higher stage of development until his brain has matured beyond the stage at which it is currently operating. He proposed that maturation (simply growing up) plays a key role in the development of a child's cognitive abilities.

According to this view, children are incapable of achieving tasks, which are currently above their developmental level until their brains have matured in accordance with that level. This view also holds that development through maturation of the brain is required before learning can take place. This view of development leaves little hope for brain-injured children whose brains' will in some cases never simply 'mature' on their own, to higher stages of development; - Thankfully, it is ***incorrect!***

Lev Vygotsky on the other hand, did not subscribe to Piaget's view. Vygotsky proposed that children's learning is social in nature; he asserted that all learning first takes place on a level which is external to the child, in social situations. As learning takes place, with assistance from more skilled others, (in this case the parents), abilities which the child could not initially perform alone are ***internalised*** to become part of the repertoire of skills of the child. In this way, learning leads development! This view gives great hope for brain-injured children. All we need to do is to determine the child's actual developmental level, - determine their 'zone of proximal development' (their next developmental level) and design activities which can help them achieve the next, higher developmental abilities. (It might be easier if you think of the ZPD as the 'zone of ***next*** development. – It is the developmental abilities which lie just out of the child's reach, but which he can achieve with appropriate training and instruction)

Let us consider what Vygotsky proposed in a little more detail, as it underpins my approach towards combating your child's learning difficulties. Lev Vygotsky was a Russian psychologist who was born in 1896 and died at thirty-eight years of age. His views on child development are only just beginning to become common currency in the Western world where the education system and child developmental viewpoint has been dominated by the views of Jean Piaget and others. Vygotsky concentrated his research upon the way in which children learn in natural situations. As the developmental level of most of our children will be at pre-school levels, we shall begin there.

In the pre-school years, children learn and parents teach (without even being aware of the fact that they are doing so), in the relaxed setting of the home and wider community, within interactions where more skilled members of family, friends and community assist in guiding their learning. This way of learning is natural and uncontrived. It involves the use of the ***sociocultural tool of language*** as a means of developing a social mode of thinking.

- **T*he sociocultural tool of language:*** *- By this, I simply mean that in such a learning situation, it is spoken language, which facilitates the interaction. This spoken language is 'external' (out in the open) and helps to make the thought processes of both parent and child available to the other. In this way the child can utilise the parent's language in order to guide his learning and the parent can utilise the child's language to understand the difficulties he may be facing and to adjust the level of assistance accordingly. In this way language becomes a social mode of thought between parent and child.*

There is evidence that this sort of language use and the consequent development of vocabulary power in young children leads to later scholastic advancement. - In this sense, learning occurs through talking! It is recognised that this type of social, learning situation encourages pre-school children to instigate interactions, ask questions and seek information eagerly. They consequently become active in their own learning and are able to utilise other people in their environment to help them. (Corson, 1988; Wood, 1986; Mercer, 1995). If this is the natural way in which children learn, then this is the way to pursue learning in brain-injured children.

Let's take an even closer look! Bruner coined the term ***scaffolding*** to define just this type of supported learning, which has been observed in children's homes; - learning which takes place through what Vygotsky termed the ***zone of proximal development***. This is a situation where the learning, which is being supported through the guidance and support of a more skilled 'other' (the support given by the parent being the scaffold), is slightly in advance of the child's current capability to carry on successfully alone. As the child's ability to carry out a task increases, the verbal and practical support and guidance given is gradually decreased, leading to a situation where the new ability becomes ***internalised*** as part of the child's developmental capability.

The concept of scaffolding was later, further refined by Rogoff, who described such supported learning as a process of ***guided participation***. The concept of 'guided participation,' emphasises not only the cognitive support given by the adult, but also acknowledges the active participation of the child in the learning process. (Rogoff et al, 1993).

There is evidence to illustrate the success of guided participation between mothers and children and although this is mainly gained from studies of mothers and children in middle class European and North American culture, there is also support that the use of guided participation is cross-cultural. (Rogoff, 1990).

Research into the areas of conceptual development, object exploration, puzzle construction and memory tasks, all demonstrate that when the dyad of mother and child colluded in these tasks, utilising a 'guided participation' approach, children advanced their skills in these areas.

(Deloach, 1983; Rogoff et al, 1984; Bornstein, 1988).

A good example is provided by one study in particular, which demonstrates that the dynamic and helpful participation of an adult in children's investigation of new objects, led to more exploration by three to seven – year – olds, than did the straightforward company of an adult. (Henderson, 1984a, 1984b).

These results indicate that this is indeed one way in which children learn, but let us take a closer look at the 'zone of proximal development,' and how new skills are attained through it until they become a part of the child's actual developmental abilities. Consider a child who is trying to learn a new skill, which he is unable to complete alone. He needs the assistance of an adult and he is totally dependent upon that adult in order to complete the task. He is just beginning his journey through the zone of proximal development, which has four stages as follows.

Stage 1: At this early stage in the learning process, a more skilled adult provides assistance in the new task. The child is totally dependent upon the guidance (the scaffold), which is provided by the adult and is unable to undertake the task alone. At this point, the ability to complete the task is ***external*** to the child; - it is within the social interaction between the child and adult.

Stage 2: Because of the guidance, which has been provided by the parent within the social learning situation, the child is able mostly to complete the task alone. In other words, the scaffolding of guidance has been gradually removed as the child's ability to carry out the task increases. At the end of this stage, the child is able to complete the task alone. At this point, the ability to complete the task is no longer external, within the social interaction between child and adult, but has been ***internalised*** by the child. The ability needed to perform the task has gone from being within the developmental grasp of the child, to actually being part of his developmental abilities.

Stage 3: Automatisation through practice. Although the child has internalised the abilities required to complete the task, they are still not firmly embedded. He may still have to use his full concentration to perform the task, even utilising language to talk himself through the process. In this way, through language which is first spoken externally and which is later spoken internally, as ***'inner speech,'*** or '***verbal thought'*** he is providing his own guidance or scaffolding. With sufficient practice, the task is gradually performed more fluently and he has to concentrate less and less in order to complete the task, until eventually, it becomes automatic.

Stage 4: De-automatisation; recursiveness through previous three stages. This happens sometimes, if the learned task is not carried out for some time, or it has not been automatised through sufficient practice. We begin again at stage 1. (Tharp & Gallimore, 1988)

The way in which children with brain-injury learn is no different to the way uninjured children learn. They are both children! The learning of one is merely obstructed by the barriers constructed by the brain-injury. We have to find a way of overcoming those barriers and the way to do this is to break down the task to be learned into subgroups of much simpler tasks, which are achievable. For instance, if you were trying to teach your child how to feed himself, would you just give him the spoon and expect him to copy you, - to follow your lead? With an uninjured child, this would be possible, but to a child with brain-injuries, this task may be as difficult to him as flying a space shuttle would be to us!

We must break the task down into a series of achievable sub-tasks. The first sub-task might be learning to hold the spoon correctly, which eventually would lead on to the second sub-task of dipping the spoon into the food. The third sub-task would then be to bring the spoonful of food back to the mouth to be eaten. Each of these sub-tasks would be learned by using the principles of the four stages of the zone of proximal development.

It might not necessarily be a practical task like learning to feed oneself that could be treated in this way; most other developmental tasks can be treated in a similar manner. No matter how severe the child's problems are, he is still capable of learning if the material is presented at the appropriate level and in an appropriate format. We just have to know where to start and how fast to progress.

In this way, we are promoting brain plasticity by using natural teaching and learning to help the child minimise his learning difficulties. So, without divulging the intricacies of the activities within a programme of developmental stimulation, (which would be difficult anyway because each programme is individually tailored to a child's needs), let's look at some of the more generalised things that parents can do to create a good developmental environment, (which will drive brain plasticity in the desired direction) for their children.

What can I do to help my child? - The power of music to influence the brain.

The potency of music and its effect on memory is quite astonishing. Baroque music and Gregorian chant in particular, with a 60 beats per minute beat pattern, have been shown to activate both the left and right hemispheres of the brain. The simultaneous left and right brain action has a beneficial effect on hemispheric coordination, learning and retention of information. If we study whilst listening to music, the information being studied activates the left brain, while the music activates the right brain. Activities which engage both sides of the brain simultaneously cause the brain to be more capable of processing information.

It is claimed that learning potential can be increased a minimum of five times by using this 60 beats per minute music. For example, the ancient Greeks sang their dramas because they understood how music could help them remember more easily.

A renowned Bulgarian psychologist, Dr. George Lozanov, designed a way to teach foreign languages in a fraction of the normal learning time. Using his system, students could learn up to one half of the vocabulary and phrases for the whole school term (which amounts to almost 1,000 words or phrases) in one day. Along with this, the average retention rate of his students was 92%. Dr. Lozanov's system involved using certain classical music pieces from the baroque period which have around a 60 beats per minute pattern. He demonstrated that foreign languages could be learned with 85-100% efficiency in a dramatically shorter time period, by using these baroque pieces. His students had a recall accuracy rate of almost 100% even after not reviewing the material for four years.

In 1982, researchers from the University of North Texas performed a three-way test on postgraduate students to see if music could help in memorizing vocabulary words. The students were divided into three groups. Each group was given three tests - a pre-test, a post test, and a test a week after the first two tests. All of the tests were identical. Group 1 was read the words with Handel's Water Music in the background. They were also asked to imagine the words. Group 2 was read the same words also with Handel's Water Music in the background. Group 2 was not asked to imagine the words. Group 3 was only read the words, was not given any background music, and was also not asked to imagine the words. The results from the first two tests showed that groups 1 and 2 had much better scores than group 3. The results from the third test, a week later, showed that group 1 performed much better than groups 2 or 3.

In another study by Särkämö et al, (2007), with patients who had suffered brain injury, it was discovered that music, when applied during the most dynamic period of recovery from neural damage, can induce long-term changes on cognition that are indexed by enhanced recovery of focused attention and verbal memory. Interestingly, the facilitating effect of music on focused attention was more pronounced in patients with damage to the language-dominant hemisphere of the brain. They also conclude that current evidence suggests that music has a rather general, non-specific effect on cognition. This is in line with the arousal and mood hypothesis (Thompson et al., 2001), which states that any enjoyable stimuli, such as music, that induces positive affect and heightened arousal can lead to improved performance on cognitive tasks

Listening to pleasant music activates an interconnected network of subcortical and cortical brain regions, which together, are crucial for mediating arousal, emotion, reward, motivation, memory, attention and executive functioning (Ashby et al., 1999). Listening to music it seems, leads to increased dopamine synthesis in the brain. Dopamine mediates alertness, speed of information processing, attention, and memory, (Schück et al., 2002), and also global cognitive functioning in patients with cognitive impairment, (Nagaraja and Jayashree, 2001). It is, thus, possible that the music-related enhanced cognitive recovery seen in this study was mediated by positive mood induced by music, and hence the dopaminergic mesocorticolimbic system.

Importantly, exposure to music also enhances brain plasticity by increasing neurogenesis in the hippocampus (Kim et al., 2006), modifying the expression of glutamate receptor GluR2 in the auditory cortex and in the anterior cingulate (Xu et al., 2007), increasing brain-derived neurotrophic factor (BDNF) levels in the hippocampus (Angelucci et al., 2007a) and in the hypothalamus

(Angelucci et al., 2007b), and also increasing the levels of tyrosine kinase receptor B (TrkB), a BDNF receptor, in the cortex (Chikahisa et al., 2006).

All of this knowledge has profound implications for the teaching and rehabilitative efforts with children who suffer a range of learning and developmental difficulties, such as autism, cerebral palsy and others and the practice of including music as part of any developmental programme is always utilised by Snowdrop.

What can I do to help my child? - The importance of exposure to speech, rhyme, alliteration and stories.

Often, it is the simple things which are most effective. In one of the previous sections when I discussed language development, we spoke about how the normal patterns of interaction break down and so language development fails to develop. Well, taking those thoughts one stage further, the breakdown often leads to the child not being exposed to nursery rhymes, which contain rhyme and alliteration and to stories. Exposure to these things is a vital component in developing a child's 'phonological awareness,' (His understanding of the sound system of the language into which he is born) and have been proven to be vital tools both in helping to develop spoken language and literacy.

If there were one thing I could say to all parents of children who have brain injuries it would be to not forget to keep saying the nursery rhymes, stories and songs!

Parents need to start talking to their child from the day he is born. Some parents are naturally quiet and reserved. Others have the disastrous impression that it is crazy to talk to their babies, knowing that they do not comprehend. The parent, who does not talk persistently while feeding, bathing and dressing their baby, is setting the stage for a late talker, or in the case of our brain injured child, a non – talker!

Children learn language in one way only, and that is by hearing it as the parents talk and talk to it. The more a parent can speak to a child, often repeating the same words, the same phrases, the same structures over and over, as we do in nursery rhymes, songs and stories, the sooner the child will learn language.

The key is repetition. Parents should read to their children as often as possible, but the secret, which will lead to optimal language development, is to read the SAME stories over and over again, to say the same nursery rhymes over and over, to sing the same songs, over and over!

In days gone by there was not the profusion of storybooks that there is today. Parents were constrained in their choice - it was also part of the child-rearing customs - to repeat to their children the few stories that they knew, or to repeatedly read to their children the few books in their possession. They also spent a lot of time teaching their children rhymes and songs. This was extremely beneficial for the acquisition of language.

What can I do to help my child? - Massage.

Massage has a proven beneficial effect upon brain function and the good news is, it doesn't have to be a professional massage, provided by a qualified masseur so that cuts down the cost! All you need to do is to make gentle skin contact using an oil or cream to which your child will not react badly and just gently massage him, just as if you are moisturising his skin. This can help muscle tone, anxiety, (you would be surprised at the number of children who are highly anxious), and can help distortions of sensory processing in the tactile modality.

The evidence for the positive effects of massage can be seen in the study carried out on ten new-borns with a gestational age between 30 and 33 weeks, admitted to the Neonatal Intensive Care Unit (NICU) of the University Hospital of Pisa, who were selected for the study on the basis of very precise conditions, to exclude confounding factors. Obviously ten new-borns matched for age, sex, and birth weight were selected according to the same criteria as controls.

In the group who received massage data indicated that enriching the environment in terms of body massage affects brain development and in particular visual system maturation in human babies. The researchers concluded that;

"*This supports the importance of massage per se in promoting brain development. These results also support the hypothesis that the level of tactile stimulation provided is an important regulator of brain development.*" Guzzetta et al, (2009)

What can I do to help my child? – Nutrition.

As important as the information which you make available to the brain through stimulation is the maintenance of the internal environment in which the brain functions. A good internal environment, where there are good levels of oxygen and nutrients will help the brain to achieve optimal functioning and thereby help to ameliorate some of the symptoms of injury. I have already mentioned fish oil supplements in relation to cognitive development, which I believe is so important as to merit its own section, but let's take a look at nutrition generally.

Numerous studies over the past 40 years have evaluated the impact of nutrition in early life on central nervous system development. These studies have clearly demonstrated that reductions in energy and/or essential nutrient supply during the first stages of life have profound effects on somatic growth, and on the structural and functional development of the brain.

The timing and nature of the nutritional insult affects brain development in different ways. For example, cell number as measured by DNA content is affected by intrauterine and early postnatal malnutrition, while synaptic connectivity can be affected if malnutrition occurs between birth and 3 years of age.

Similarly, variations in the supply of dietary precursors may determine neurotransmitter levels (serotonin, norepinephrine, dopamine, and acetylcholine), while variation in the supply of essential and nonessential lipids may affect the structural composition of the brain and of myelin sheaths. It has also become clear that brain somatic growth may proceed normally in the face of certain nutritional insults (such as those caused by iron and taurine), but that brain structure and function are significantly altered if specific essential nutrients are lacking during development.

It is clear from the research of Uauy et al that to encourage optimal brain development in early life, starting at or most likely before conception, should include the provision of key micronutrients including folate, retinol, iodine, iron, zinc, and copper, all of which are necessary to support neurogenesis during embryonic and foetal development.

In infancy and childhood, preventing iodine, iron, and zinc deficiency while avoiding exposure to neurotoxic elements such as lead and other heavy metals is key in achieving full potential cognitive capacity and unnecessary loss of mental capacity.

We now know that micronutrient sufficiency and quality of the lipid supply play key roles in brain development. Loss of intellectual function linked to iodine deficiency remains the most frequent preventable cause of mental retardation globally. Usuy et al. (http://200.89.70.78:8080/jspui/bitstream/2250/6314/1/Uauy_Ricardo.pdf).

So, what to do? Breast milk offers the best mix of nutrients for promoting brain growth, provided that breast-fed infants receive some form of iron supplementation beginning around six months of age. (Most infant cereals are fortified with iron, and breast-fed babies require this supplementation at six months whether or not their mothers are iron-deficient.) Iron deficiency has been clearly linked to cognitive deficits in young children. Iron is critical for maintaining an adequate number of oxygen-carrying red blood cells, which in turn are necessary to fuel brain growth. Bottle-fed babies should receive formula that contains iron.

Because of the rapid pace of myelination in early life, children need a high level of fat in their diets--some 50 per cent of their total calories--until about two years of age. Babies should receive most of this fat from breast milk or formula in the first year of life, and breast milk remains an excellent source of liquid nutrition into the toddler years. However, whole cow's milk can be introduced after the first birthday, and provides an excellent source of both fat and protein for toddlers in the second year. After two years of age, children should begin transitioning to a more heart-healthy level of dietary fat.

As the child progresses on to solid foods, protein from dairy products, meats, nuts, fish, and vegetables like cabbage and cauliflower, carbohydrates from pasta, breads and cereals, are readily available and should be part of a well-balanced daily diet. As the next section discusses, omega 3 fatty acids found in oily fish are especially beneficial to the developing brain.

Fish oils and cognition.

We have all 'known for a long time the benefits of Omega 3 Fish oil supplementation, but it is always nice when a piece of research comes along which gives validity to this 'knowledge. Thanks to the Guardian for pointing this one out, - It has been implemented into Snowdrop programmes of rehabilitation for brain injured children immediately.

Children can learn better at school by taking omega-3 fish oil supplements which boost their concentration, scientists say.

Boys aged eight to 11 who were given doses once or twice a day of docosahexaenoic acid, an essential fatty acid known as DHA, showed big improvements in their performance during tasks involving attention.

Dr Robert McNamara, of the University of Cincinnati, who led the team of American researchers, said their findings could help pupils to study more effectively and potentially help to tackle both attention deficit hyperactivity disorder (ADHD) and depression. The study, reported in the American Journal of Clinical Nutrition, is important because a lack of DHA has been implicated in ADHD and other similar conditions, with poor maternal diet sometimes blamed for the child's deficiency.

ADHD affects an estimated 4%-8% of Britons and can seriously impair a child's education because they have trouble concentrating and are often disruptive in class. A lack of DHA has also been associated with bipolar disorder and schizophrenia.

"We found that, if you take DHA, you can enhance the function of those brain regions that are involved in paying attention, so it helps people concentrate," said McNamara. "The benefit is that it may represent an intervention that will help children or adults with attention impairments."

The researchers gave 33 US schoolboys 400mg or 1,200mg doses of DHA or a placebo every day for eight weeks. Those who had received the high doses did much better in mental tasks involving mathematical challenges. Brain scans showed that functional activity in their frontal cortex – which controls memory, attention and the ability to plan – increased significantly.

The results, and fact that many people eat too little fish to get enough DHA through their diet, meant it could help all children to improve their learning, added McNamara. "The primary benefit is to treat ADHD and depression, but it could also help people with their memory, learning and attention," he said.

What can I do to help my child? – Meditation.

I can hear some of you laughing now, thinking. "How can I get my child to meditate, he can't keep still for more than a second," or "he doesn't understand what I am saying to him" and it is true, this is a technique which can only be used on some children, but when it is used successfully it can have some very positive results. The meditative episode needs only to be a short length in duration to begin with, literally a few seconds at a time. Over the weeks and months, this can be built upon, second by second, minute by minute.

Meditation has produced some remarkable results with both children and adults who suffer ADHD, but its use should not be just limited to this condition as it has been proven to produce positive structural changes in the brain. http://www.crystalinks.com/medbrain.html

Everyone should meditate, but particularly, children and adults who have brain injuries should meditate and those who are suitable candidates for instruction are taught to do so as part of their Snowdrop programme.

Epilepsy.

Epilepsy is a very common problem in brain-injured children. It is very distressing to watch and can be debilitating for the child. It is also exceptionally varied, ranging from a few unnatural blinks of the eye through to a 'whole body' convulsion. Just when I think, I have witnessed probably just about every variety of epileptic attack, up pops a child who produces something unique.

What is epilepsy?

Epilepsy is the tendency of specific brain-cells to misfire. There are three distinctions of epilepsy to bear in mind in understanding this problem. The first distinction is that an epileptic episode is either ***partial*** or ***generalised***. The second distinction is that an epileptic episode is either ***simple*** or ***complex.*** The third distinction is that epileptic seizures are either ***grand mal*** or ***petit mal***. Confused? – Don't worry, read on and it will all become clear.

Normally, brain cells fire according to their being excited beyond a certain threshold of stimulation, or they are restrained from firing because they are inhibited from doing so. Sometimes in epilepsy, these inhibition and excitation thresholds are not applied successfully, causing brain cells to misfire very easily. When this happens, two things can occur:

1. The misfiring may be limited to a specific area of the brain, causing a very specific response from the individual such as a short ***absence*** or a twitching of one limb. These are known as ***partial*** seizures.

2. The misfiring may form a chain reaction, which spreads to a larger area of the brain, causing a more ***generalised*** response from the brain. Adams & Victor (1981) successfully demonstrated this phenomenon by measuring seizure activity with electrodes placed inside patients' brains. (In Ropper, et al, 2000).

Partial seizures can be further subdivided by our second distinction of ***simple*** and ***complex***.

Simple, partial seizures bring about changes in the level of consciousness, but never involve a loss of consciousness, whereas ***complex partial seizures*** do involve a loss of consciousness.

Sometimes, if the focus of the epileptic activity is in one of the ***temporal lobes*** of the brain, the child may experience an ***aura*** prior to the attack. This 'aura' may be an experience of positive or negative emotions, it may be a hallucination of one or more sensory modality, or the aura may trigger memories or stereotypical movements.

We now come to our third distinction of seizure activity, ***grand mal*** and ***petit mal*** seizures. Sometimes during a more dramatic 'complex partial' seizure, the child's body may rhythmically shake. This is known as a ***grand mal*** or ***tonic - clonic*** seizure. Although this looks dramatic, it is nothing to be alarmed about and is usually over within a few minutes as a combination of structures in the brain, collectively known as the ***diencephalon*** act to suppress the seizure activity.

A ***petit mal*** seizure is less dramatic, usually very brief and is sometimes so shallow as to go unnoticed by parents, teachers and doctors. An example of such a seizure would be an ***absence,*** where the child simply stares vacantly for a second or two. I know a child who used to experience more than fifty such absences an hour and although they sound unobtrusive, when experienced at this magnitude the disruptive effect they can have upon life is easily underestimated.

Finally, and importantly, one aspect of epileptic activity, which it is important to discuss is a phenomenon known as ***status epilepticus***. Usually seizure activity will dissipate within a few minutes and the child will recover with no harm done. However, rarely the seizure activity either will not stop, or the child emerges from one seizure, quickly to be consumed by another and another. This is a dangerous and potentially life threatening situation, which needs immediate medical intervention. In extreme cases such as this, seizures are capable of causing further brain-damage.

It has been demonstrated that some patients with seizure disorders display injury to a part of the brain called the ***hippocampus***, the amount of damage being closely correlated with the number and severity of seizures, which the patient has experienced. The damage appears to be caused by the excessive release of a neurochemical called ***glutamate*** during the seizure. (Thompson et al, 1996). It is consequently vital that even if you only suspect your child to be experiencing seizure activity, that this is checked out and treated by a doctor.

What causes epilepsy?

Epilepsy has two causes, one is ***pathological,*** and the second is ***physiological*** in nature.

- Pathology: -When a brain suffers injury, millions of brain cells may die. Around the area of injury, there may also be cells, which have not been killed, but which are nevertheless injured. In addition, as I have previously alluded, the thresholds of excitation and inhibition, which normally control the firing of these cells, may have been disrupted. Therefore, these injured cells may not fire according to their normal patterns, but may more or less constantly misfire. The child in this situation may have more or less constant epileptic activity occurring in his brain.

- Physiology: - The environment in which the brain operates is by necessity oxygen and nutrient rich. Although the brain only comprises approximately 2% of the body's weight, it consumes 25% of the body's oxygen intake. When a brain suffers injury, the availability of the oxygen supply can be compromised. For instance, in many cases of brain-injury, the development of the rate and depth of breathing of the child, does not progress from that of a new-born, which is fast and shallow; - this places difficulties on the optimum levels of oxygen availability, thereby compromising the physiological environment of the brain. Similarly, uninjured children who are ill and develop a temperature may suffer an epileptic seizure as the temperature rise deprives the brain of oxygen, temporarily creating a poor physiological environment.

The young child with brain-injuries may also have trouble in taking in adequate nutrition, which could cause similar physiological effects. The brain's response to this impoverished physiological environment is to produce a seizure reaction. When brain cells struggle to operate normally without the oxygen and the nutrition they need, they begin to misfire.

What can be done to combat epilepsy?

There are many approaches to combating epilepsy which may improve your child's situation. Often a programme of developmental stimulation can reduce seizure activity. The reason for this is that if developmental gains can be produced in the child, it means the brain is operating at a more mature, efficient level. This 'brain development' can suppress seizure activity.

It is also important that children, who are predisposed towards epilepsy, be given good nutrition. This will help to maintain the physiological environment of the brain in as optimal a state as possible and hopefully keep seizure activity to a minimum.

There is a wealth of medical technology now available, which can help to combat seizure activity. Anti-convulsant medication always extracts a price from the child in terms of drowsiness and other side effects, but it is often necessary, if only temporarily to keep epilepsy under control. As long as the levels of medication are kept to the minimum needed to control the seizure, there is no harm in pursuing this path.

How do I get on programme and what does a programme involve?

The easiest way to get started is to telephone, email, or write using the information given at the back of this book. It sounds easy doesn't it? I do realise that it is not. I know it is difficult to pick up the telephone, or to compose that email or letter because it is a big step. It is an admission that things aren't working, - that to your perception, the system has failed. It is a very difficult and a very courageous thing to do to step outside that system. Let me ease your worries a little, because although I might be providing something different from what is on offer through the health system, I am very much accepted by that system.

All my qualifications come from mainstream universities in the UK. I am an accepted member of the British Institute of Learning Disabilities and the British Academy of Childhood Disability, - both mainstream institutions in the UK. I can be found through links from the NHS 'choices' website and the directory of the National Autistic Society, both of which I am sure you will agree are reputable institutions 'within the system.' So don't make that call or write that email thinking that the system will react in a hostile manner to your stepping outside it, - it won't. Although I am providing something which the system does not offer, what I do provide, - the techniques I use can be referenced via mainstream psychology and child development sources.

What does a programme involve?

The answer to this question depends upon two factors, - (1). The child and the problems he displays; - (2). The family and the problems they might have with incorporating the programme into everyday life.

As far as the child is concerned, I will generally prescribe a programme of developmental activities which will last for two hours per day, to be carried out for five days per week. However, some children display problems with sensory over-sensitivity and will react very badly to a programme of this intensity, indeed in such cases; such an intense programme could worsen the child's problems. In these cases, a gently, gently approach is justified and a much lighter programme is prescribed whilst we try to resolve the over-sensitivity issues.

As far as the family are concerned, our priority is to support them in what they can do, not overwhelm them in trying to do what for them, in their particular circumstances would be impossible.

The programme itself consists of a set of activities, which will mostly last one or two minutes, - or occasionally five minutes, which are repeated several times per day (we have seen the evidence earlier on how the brain's inherent quality of plasticity responds to repetition). Some of these exercises will be sensory in nature; some will focus on mobility, language, socialisation, hand function and cognition.

Some families, especially those following the more intensive approach, like to recruit volunteers to help carry out the child's programme. This is fine, it helps to give the family a break and can make life more interesting and varied for both the child and the family. Some families prefer to keep the programme within the family; - this is also fine although the repetitive nature of the exercises can be wearing if you are doing the programme alone.

Which children are suitable or unsuitable candidates for treatment?

There is no child with any type or severity of brain injury that Snowdrop does not offer treatment for. If your child has been labelled with one of the following symptomatic terms, we will do all we can help you.

ADHD, agenesis of the corpus callosum, agnosia, Angelman's syndrome, aphasia, apraxia, Asperger's syndrome, ataxia, athetosis, autism, brain injury, brain damage, cerebral palsy, Dandy – Walker syndrome, developmental delay, diplegia, dysgenesis of the corpus callosum, dysgraphia, dyslexia, dyspraxia, dystonia, epilepsy, hemiplegia, hemiparesis, hydrocephalus, hypertonia, hypotonia., learning difficulties, locked in syndrome, microcephaly, quadriplegia, Rett syndrome, spasticity, stroke, traumatic brain injury, tremor, West syndrome, Worster – Drought syndrome.

These are just the major areas of neuro-developmental problems I provide programmes for. I am aware that there are more. Suffice it to say that if your child's problems are neurological in cause, then I will attempt to provide you with a programme of stimulation.

Parents as therapists

It is my belief that parents make the best therapists. As a parent myself who carried out various programmes with my own child, I have experienced this truth. Parents know their child better than anyone; - better than any physiotherapist can ever know him, better than any doctor can ever know him and certainly better than I can ever know him. Parents are more motivated to help their child than anyone else could ever possibly be, - that is why they are the best people to be doing or supervising their child's programme.

The proof of this is now solid. Dr Marie Arsalidou, from the University of Toronto, in Canada has produced research which demonstrates that mothers produce complex and lasting emotional and cognitive responses in their children's brain, as a result of the bonding experience that takes place between them and their children, as babies. (http://www.telegraph.co.uk/science/science-news/7969398/Mum-matters-most-in-the-eyes-of-their-children.html).

When a baby is born who has neurological problems and he is brought home, we know that normal patterns of interaction between baby and parents often break down. This next study shows that this must have a further negative impact upon brain development. This is why a Snowdrop programme which stimulates communication always includes 'back to basics' activities to overcome this and stimulate brain development.

UCI child neurologist and neuroscientist Dr. Tallie Z. Baram has found that maternal care and other sensory input triggers activity in a baby's developing brain that improves cognitive function and builds resilience to stress.

For an infant, a mother's touch provides a feeling of security, comfort and love. But research at UC Irvine is showing that it does much more.

UCI child neurologist and neuroscientist Dr. Tallie Z. Baram has found that caressing and other sensory input triggers activity in a baby's developing brain that improves cognitive function and builds resilience to stress.

The finding contributes to growing knowledge about epigenetics, the study of how environmental factors can reprogram the expression of genes.

In a study published earlier this year in The Journal of Neuroscience, Baram and colleagues identified how sensory stimuli from maternal care can modify genes that control a key messenger of stress called corticotrophin-releasing hormone.

In earlier work, Baram helped discover that excessive amounts of CRH in the brain's primary learning and memory centre led to the disintegration of dendritic spines, branchlike structures on neurons. Dendritic spines facilitate the sending and receiving of messages among brain cells and the collection and storage of memories.

"Communication among brain cells is the foundation of cognitive processes such as learning and memory," says Baram, the Danette Shepard Chair in Neurological Sciences. "In several brain disorders where learning and similar thought processes are abnormal, dendritic spines have been found to be reduced in density or poorly developed.

"Because an infant's brain is still building connections in these communication zones, large blasts or long-term amounts of stress can permanently limit full development, increasing the risk of anxiety, depression and dementia later in life."

Her most recent study describes for the first time the cellular pathways of the epigenetic process by which maternal care reduces the expression of CRH in the hypothalamus. Detecting sensory input, DNA in brain cells in this stress-sensitive region activates a neuron-restrictive silencer factor, which limits CRH. Without the interference of excess stress-triggered CRH, neural dendrites in the hippocampus can fully develop, which leads to stress resilience.

"What's noteworthy about this study is that it reveals that brain structure is influenced by the environment early in life, and especially by maternal care," says Baram, whose research on early-life factors in neural development has fundamentally altered the understanding of disorders such as epilepsy.

"There has been a belief that the brain is hardwired - that once it's established, it's that way for life," she says. "But we're seeing that the brain is actually 'soft wired' - that changes in stimuli alter the wiring - and that it's not predestined to be a certain way. I find this fascinating."

This research proves that parents and in particular mothers undoubtedly make the best therapists for Snowdrop programmes.

Teamwork

It is very easy to lose sight of your child as a person when you are immersed in the purpose of trying to solve your child's problems and you are planning and carrying out a schedule of developmental stimulation. As the old aphorism states: - *It is very difficult, when up to one's ears in Alligators, to remember that one's original intention was to drain the swamp!*

Should you decide to embark on any type of therapeutic intervention, you should consider carefully just what you are trying to achieve. Brain-injury cannot be cured! It certainly cannot be cured by me (although the overwhelming majority of my children make good progress) and I do not know of any other clinic anywhere in the world that would make such a claim. If they do, you should run out of the door as fast as possible!

What we can do between us, parents and therapist working as a team is to provide the best possible developmental environment for your child, which will enable him to make the maximum degree of progress. In doing so, care has to be taken that a situation is not created, which is making too heavy a level of demand upon the family. If this situation is allowed to develop, the programme becomes absolute drudgery for both the family and the child. The quality of stimulation being provided is then very poor. This kind of situation is also one where the identity of the child can be lost. The child can become almost an object, to which things are done! This is counterproductive not only to the child's developmental opportunities, but that it places unnecessary stress upon already overburdened families.

If you ever feel you are losing sight of the wonderful individual underneath all the developmental stimulation you are providing; - your child, then you are trying too hard and could create a counterproductive environment. In this case, it is time for a re-think!

The most important aspect of your child's life is ***YOU.*** The relationship you build with your child, the love you give him and the love you receive back, will build a platform on which those initial interactions, which are the precursors to so much developmental progress, can begin.

What we are trying to achieve is 'happy families.' Only if the family is happy, relaxed and fully understanding of what they are trying to achieve, will the injured child respond in a manner, which is likely to encourage the building of his relationships with other members of the family. Only then, through those relationships of trust, mutual affection and the enjoyment of interaction can we begin the journey down the developmental pathway.

Parent – professional and family relations

A major problem faced by many parents, whether they pursue alternative treatments or not, is the response to the family of the healthcare professionals. Many parents report negative experiences in dealing with professionals, especially if they are following a course of action with which the professional disagrees. One family reported an incident to us, which frankly is typical!

Their trouble began with a physiotherapist who regularly visited their home to treat their four-year-old son, who suffered from profound brain-injury. Soon after they had begun a programme of developmental stimulation, - a situation by which this particular therapist obviously felt threatened, she began to make derogatory comments about the fact that their son would occasionally incur a minor rub or bruise from trying to crawl down his wooden ramp. This is a situation, which is unfortunate, but it occasionally happens. It is usually remedied by a slight alteration in the angle of the ramp to the floor. The bruises were not frequent or severe and one would expect a well, uninjured toddler to pick up such bruises in the course of stumbling about the house. At first, the parents studiously made no response to the remarks, but the increasing malevolence of the words was building to a crescendo. The 'tipping point' occurred when, at the end of one visit the therapist disparagingly said *"I wonder what social services would make of those marks on Gareth's leg?"* This was simply too much for the family to take and they confronted the therapist, asking precisely what point she was trying to make. As is always the case with bullies, the moment they are confronted, or asked to justify their words, they 'turn tail' and run! As she quickly disappeared through the door, she mumbled something about 'joking' and not taking her seriously. She apparently never uttered another remark about Gareth's minor scrapes.

Yet another confrontation between one of my clients and the ranks of the 'professionals' emerged when a new paediatrician asked a particular family to pay her a visit in her office, as she wished to get to know their daughter and become acquainted with her problems. (At least this was what the doctor stated on the telephone!) She gave the impression of being supportive towards the family and appeared to be genuinely interested in what they were trying to achieve for their daughter. Suitably lulled into a false sense of security, the parents happily took their daughter, Julie along to see the doctor. However, when they arrived in her office, she told them plainly that she fundamentally disagreed with what they were doing in terms of therapy and what was more, were they to continue, she would "*not touch Julie with a barge pole*!" The family simply could not believe the complete turnaround in the woman's attitude and asked her to tell them precisely what it was about Julie's therapy that offended her so much. Of course, as has been the case with every single member of the medical profession I have encountered, she was unable to substantiate her view with any evidence. - She was unable to say what she found disagreeable because she did not actually ***know*** anything about what it was she so violently disagreed with!

Again, as is typical of many 'professionals' I have encountered, she was merely reacting to rumour and hearsay generated from within her profession and being the unimaginative sheep, which some of them undoubtedly are, their opinion must mirror that of the flock! Why allow truth, fact and evidence to spoil good prejudicial opinion?

The woman then continued to accuse the family of being ***"on a high"*** stating that her perception was that they seemed to be ***enjoying*** their daughter's disabilities! What kind of twisted, warped personality could imagine that parents would enjoy their child's difficulties? In this particular case, all the family were trying to do was to undo the harm, which had been inflicted upon Julie through medical negligence at birth; - medical negligence fostered by just this kind of conceited arrogance.

The most horrific incident, of which I am aware, involved my own family and a 'professional' and was played out in our absence, but was reported to us by a friend. Just prior to our son beginning a programme of developmental activities, we had moved away from our old neighbourhood to an area approximately fifteen miles from where our son had been born. Obviously, via the 'professional' grapevine, news our family embarking upon a different type of therapy had travelled back to where we formerly lived and other parents of children with developmental disabilities, who attended the same clinics, which we formerly attended with our son, began asking questions about us and our new programme. One of these parents, with whom we had become friendly during our clinic visits, telephoned one evening in great concern to ask if we were both coping with the ***divorce proceedings!*** Of course, no such event was occurring at all!

Apparently, desperate that other parents did not follow in our footsteps, one 'professional' had elected to inform the other families that the new programme on which we had embarked was so stressful, it had broken up our marriage and we were in the process of going through a particularly acrimonious divorce! The friend was assured that this was not the case, that although the programme was indeed hard work, our relationship was more solid now than it had ever been.

To this day, I have difficulty believing that an adult human being, particularly one claiming to be a 'professional' in the caring services, would be so vicious and nasty. I feel these remarks were made out of fear; - a fear borne out of inadequacy at having no solutions to offer herself! A fear borne out of viewing a therapeutic intervention, which was outside her jurisdiction as a threat to her professional competence!

The professional attitude towards parents reported by parents themselves is one, which appears to be peppered with arrogance. Parents, instead of being viewed as partners and valuable information sources more often feel as though they are viewed as an integral part of the problem. Unfortunately, this means that whatever parents say will not be taken seriously, if it is listened to at all! It is probably this display of arrogance and contempt, which is instrumental in parents wanting to seek 'alternative' solutions to their children's problems in the first place. In other words doctors, it is often ***your*** attitude, which drives families away from you!

Yet another 'showdown' was reported to me when another doctor called at the home of one of our families to perform a routine, periodic developmental assessment on a child. According to the family, during his visit he did his level best to explain in his 'doctor knows best' voice, what a terrible mistake the family were making by following the developmental programme I had devised for the child. He stated that, in his opinion, this type of therapy was scientifically unfounded and simply would not work. The family asked him what it was precisely, about their son's programme that he objected to. –

Surprise, surprise, he could not provide an answer to this question as he possessed no real knowledge of what the family were doing.

He was then provided with several research papers from eminent psychologists, verifying some techniques within their son's programme, which demonstrated the validity of the approach. Faced with hard evidence, provided by reputable academics, this buffoon still tried to argue that the family were wasting their time! Notably, unlike the family carrying out our programme, he provided no evidence to substantiate ***his*** argument.

To the family's credit they pursued this point further by asking him what he thought of the prospects for their son if they decided not to do anything to help him at all, instead being prepared to leave him trapped in a body which he couldn't control? The parents stated that in their eyes they considered ***that*** approach to be cruel! Staggeringly, his response was that their son was happy enough now, so why not leave him? – This attitude says it all! I tell you this, although I harbour no criticism of parents who decide not to follow a treatment methodology with their child, there is one inescapable truth to be told: - ***Doing nothing is likely to achieve nothing!***

Surely to be a scientist, (which so many health professionals love to claim to be) means that one should approach a situation with an open mind and only be swayed by evidence; - instead this man was listening and subscribing to prejudice and hearsay.

When a family embark upon an alternative therapy programme, as long as the approach cannot cause harm to the child, their decision should be respected. Parents do not make this type of choice because they wish to elicit open confrontation, or with the aim of excluding treatment and advice from health professionals. Parents should not have to consider that anyone might be ***upset*** by their decision to turn every stone to help their child. This however is the way in which health care professionals often seem to interpret such decisions. The very people, who even if they disagree with parents, should continue to offer their support and advice, often react with nothing short of hysteria and open hostility.

In another instance, one family asked why their paediatrician had been so offensive about their chosen course of therapy for their son, Mark. The doctor replied that she disagreed with the intensity of the programme and had seen marriages broken apart by such regimes. The family pointed out that they were only working with Mark for two hours per day, which was all the time they could commit and that the activities in which they were involved were actually more akin to play sessions and were not intensive at all. They highlighted that if Mark attended school, which legally he could, he would then be exposed to a six - hour day educational programme. The paediatrician simply would not listen and the encounter ended with them asking to be referred to another doctor.

Some families become tired, bored and frustrated with the constant hostility which some 'professionals' throw in their direction. Apparently some of them act in this way because in trying their best to help their child, parents are not following the doctor's wishes. Therefore, it seems, in some cases it may be a matter of loss of power and control, not medical concern, which are the motivating factors behind medical reaction. Most parents have enough to do and enough problems to deal with, without having to put up with narrow minded criticism from so called 'professionals' who seemingly possess few solutions themselves!

In my opinion, this doctor was fundamentally wrong; - a marriage would be more likely to encounter difficulties if the couple were forced to sit back and merely watch, as their child simply did not develop at all, or even deteriorated.

It is clear by the contents of the letter written by this doctor after her visit, that what was related to her about the intensity of Mark's programme, was simply not comprehended!' This was no surprise to me at all, as I have realised from bitter experience that parents simply are not listened to!

In her letter she writes:-

"When I saw them, I expressed my extreme concern about this type of intensive physiotherapy."

Well, for a start, if she had actually read the information provided for her prior to her visit, she would have realised that the programme was absolutely nothing to do with physiotherapy, and as was explained to her it was not intensive at all!

It is clear to see in the academic literature and it is a view, which has been reinforced by every parent to whom I have ever spoken, that the major source of stress which families face is not their child's disability, but the relationship with the people who should be there to support parents: - the healthcare professionals!

As far as marital problems are concerned, there is no evidence that embarking upon a particular type of therapy with a child is likely to place a marriage under any extra duress. The most prevalent factor within the situation seems to be pre-existing stress between all members of the family, which may adversely affect family relationships. This is not caused by a type of therapy, but by the inbuilt stresses caused by the child's problems. A child who has brain-injuries, who does not sleep, has problems taking in sufficient sustenance, is difficult to handle physically and has associated behavioural, toileting and medical difficulties, will not create a situation where parents are calm relaxed and happy!

The difficulties brought about by the child's brain-injuries, (note, ***not*** by any form of therapy), can affect the way in which the parents not only react to one another, but to other family members. Most authorities agree that the presence of a child with brain-injury within a family most often has the effect of 'cementing' an already strong relationship, or breaking a weak one. One leading paediatrician to whom I spoke confirmed this view. He claimed after a few months of getting to know the family, he could usually make an accurate guess as to which relationships would not survive the ordeal. He asserted that in his experience, the presence of the child intensifies the pattern the relationship already has.

Indeed, it is unfortunate that the problems which are posed by the child's difficulties (not a therapeutic intervention), can cause considerable marital conflict and even, in some instances divorce! One of the foremost difficulties seems to be that parents simply do not have as much time to devote to each other, because the child's problems are so demanding.

Therefore, reviewing the actual ***evidence,*** it is the ***child's condition***, which causes marital stress, not any particular ***therapeutic intervention,*** which the parents may choose to follow with their child.

The ***evidence*** refutes the claim of this particular doctor that programmes such as that prescribed by Snowdrop and other clinics cause untold stress within families. It is simply not the truth! According to the ***evidence***, such stress is caused by the child's condition and the parents' relationship with healthcare professionals! Two studies in particular demonstrate that mothers of children with cerebral palsy (studies in which the children are not following any particular form of treatment!), suffer significantly more psychiatric symptoms than do 'ordinary' mothers. All you have to do is to look it up in the literature or online!

Surely, a developmental programme of the type we are discussing would help to alleviate such stress, because parents would at least feel that they were trying to achieve something positive. They would be more likely to feel that they were productively trying to help their child.

The problems, which parents encounter due to the child's condition, such as having time for each other are also transferred to interaction time with other children. Consequently, siblings may feel neglected and show jealousy towards their injured brother or sister. (Furneaux, 1988)

These are the genuine difficulties, which have been uncovered by academic research, they are not problems invented by the dreaming of a doctor, who quite simply merely wishes to stop you seeking valid alternatives for your child.

Therefore, contrary to medical opinion, Snowdrop type programmes are likely to decrease the social isolation and stress felt within families of children with brain-injuries.

An interesting study, commissioned in the nineties, cross–referenced the psychological well-being of siblings with the amount of interaction between them and their brain–injured brother or sister. The results of this research supported the theory that children who are encouraged into greater interaction with their injured sibling are more self–confident than children who do not receive such encouragement. It was also noted that there was an overall improvement in family interaction patterns and a functional change for the better in the child suffering from the brain–injury. (Craft, 1990). Kind of an argument for family involvement in some sort of programme isn't it?

Another major concern, which for most parents causes untold heartache, is the reaction of other people to their injured child. Parents seem to pass through definable phases in their reactions to strangers, initially wanting to talk, to tell the world all about their child. Indeed, I remember being a complete and utter bore concerning my own son. Someone would only have to mention his name to elicit a three-hour lecture on the ills of cerebral palsy!

Of course, this is not only a sign that parents feel isolated, it is also a sure sign that they need someone to talk to. It is yet another unfortunate failing of our healthcare system that often strangers have to fulfil the role of counsellor.

Later it seems, parents wish to be left alone and even resent inquiring strangers. Again, I can vouch for this as it mirrors my own experience and the experiences of many other parents to whom I have spoken. As the years passed and the problems faced by my own son became more and more visibly obvious, people would naturally look at him. I never liked this, but do understand that it is difficult not to look at someone who appears so different. The problem, with which I always grappled, was that some people would come back for a second look, or make it obvious that they were scrutinising my son. Some people simply have no idea of the distress they can cause!

So where do we go from here?

After many years as a parent of a profoundly brain-injured child, almost as many years in academic research and working in schools with children who have special educational needs, I decided the time had arrived to fulfil a long held ambition. Having travelled internationally to clinics, both as a parent and as a researcher, I have become aware of two things.

1. I became very frustrated and angry at how many alternative centres there are, both in the UK and abroad who are either promoting 'fly by night' fanciful theories concerning brain function and child development, - or are making claims and promises to parents which simply cannot be justified by their results, - or are treating children on the basis of possessing little or no qualifications to do so. There are clinics in this country, which are major national charities who fit this description.
2. I have also become aware of just how little of the vast amount of knowledge possessed by the discipline of psychology is being applied to the treatment of children with brain-injuries. Knowledge from great psychologists such as Vygotsky and Luria; from Bruner and Rogoff and from a hundred other names. The knowledge, some of which is highlighted in this book, is out there waiting to be used for the benefit of our children. I have elected to try to utilise this knowledge and apply it to the treatment of brain-injury.

I have personal experience and knowledge of the serious consequences for the family, which the presence of a child with brain-injury can bring, not least of all the problem of stress, which family members bear. As I have previously stated, a child with brain-injuries, with his myriad of associated difficulties, is likely to create tired, stressed parents, -

Understandably so! This needs to be taken into account when dealing with the family and in this sense, we are not merely treating the brain-injury, nor merely the child; - We are treating the whole family and if we are to have a significant impact upon the problems presented by brain-injury we must surely do so!

With these thoughts in mind, and having worked alongside parents and brain-injured children for many years, I have decided to establish a child development consultancy called 'Snowdrop.' (Snowdrops have a special significance for my family and our little boy). The primary focus will obviously be treatment. Snowdrop will start small, it is an idea which is in its infancy, which currently has little infrastructure or finance, but sometimes you have to just leap and build your wings on your way down!

My personal crusade will be to ensure that Snowdrop remains 'research friendly' and eclectic. By this, I mean we should not develop a set philosophy or rationale, which will affect our methodology. – Down that road lies academic egoism and inflexibility, which I have witnessed at so many other institutions and which would lead to stagnation. We should always look to research and to evidence to provide our treatment methods and not be afraid to change.

It is my hope that this short text has been informative and that most of all it has given parent some hope that their children can make progress! It is not meant to be an extended text, which delves deeply into all of the problems faced by our children and their families; - There are so many problems that it would be unwieldy and impractical to present to parents. On that basis it was intended to be relatively brief and to the point! I hope it succeeded.

Contact Details

If you are interested in using Snowdrop's services, please visit our website at http://www.snowdropcerebralpalsyandautism.com

Email us at snowdrop_cdc@btinternet.com

Write to us at the following address: -

Snowdrop Child Development Consultants.

Middle Beer

Brithem Bottom

Cullompton

Devon

EX15 1NB

Telephone us internationally on 44(0)1884 38447

Or from within the UK on 01884 38447

Contact Details

References

Angelucci F, Fiore M, Ricci E, Padua L, Sabino A, Tonali PA. Investigating the neurobiology of music: brain-derived neurotrophic factor modulation in the hippocampus of young adult mice. Behav Pharmacol 2007a;18:491-6.

Ashby FG, Isen AM, Turken AU. A neuropsychological theory of positive affect and its influence on cognition. Psychol Rev 1999; 106:529–550.

Beck, A. T., and Guthrie, T. (1956). Psychological significance of visual auras: Study of three cases with brain damage and seizures. Psychosomatic Medicin, Vol XVIII, no 2,

Berk, L. E. (1997). Child Development. (4th Edition) London. Boston. Allyn & Bacon.

Beyerstein, B. Mind-Myths: Exploring Everyday Mysteries of the Mind and Brain. New York: John Wiley and Sons, 1999.

Bobath, K., (1980). A neurophysiological basis for the treatment of cerebral palsy. London. Spastics international medical publications.

Bochner et al, 1999 in Law, M. C. Evidence based rehabilitation, a guide to practice. SLACK Incorporated; First edition (30 April 2002)ISBN-10: 1556424531

Bornstein, M. H. (1988). Mothers, infants and the development of cognitive competence. In Rogoff, B. (1990). Apprenticeship in Thinking: Cognitive Development in Social Context. Oxford. Oxford University Press.

Bruno, L. (2006). Conscious Living: How a Brain Injury Changed the Way I Make Decisions. http://www.internationalrenaissancecoaching.com/s_140.asp

Carlson, N. R. (2007). Physiology of Behavior. London. Allyn and Bacon.

Chikahisa S, Sei H, Morishima M, Sano A, Kitaoka K, Nakaya Y, et al. Exposure to music in the perinatal period enhances learning performance and alters BDNF/TrkB signaling in mice as adults. Behav Brain Res 2006;169:312-9.

Corson, D. (1988). Oral Language Across the Curriculum. Clevedon. Multilingual Matters.

Deloach, J. S. (1983). Joint picture book reading as memory training for toddlers. Paper presented at the Meeting for the society for research in child development. Detroit.

Dunn, J., Brown, J., & Beardsall, L. (1990). Family talk about feeling states and children's later understanding of others emotions. Developmental Psychology. 26.

Elbert, T. (1998). Brain Plasticity. http://www.abc.net.au/rn/talks/8.30/helthrpt/stories/s10302.htmp.

Guzzetta, A.. Baldini, S., Bancale, A., Bronncelli, A., Ciucci, F., Ghirri, F., Putignano, E., Sale, A., Viegi, A,. Berardi, N,. Boldrini, A,. Cioni, G., and Maffei, L. Massage Accelerates Brain Development and the Maturation of Visual Function. The Journal of Neuroscience, May 6, 2009, 29(18):6042-6051

Haist; F. Adamo, M. Westerfield, M. Courchesne, E. Townsend, J. The Functional Neuroanatomy of Spatial Attention in Autism Spectrum Disorder. Developmental Neuropsychology, Volume 27, Issue 3 June 2005 , pages 425 - 458

Henderson, B. B. (1984a). Parents and Exploration: The effect of context on individual differences in exploratory behaviour. Child Development. 55 1237 – 1245.

Henderson, B. B. (1984b). Social support and exploration. Child Development 55, 1246-1251.

Heywood, C. A. and Kentridge, R. W. (2003). Achromatopsia, color vision and cortex. Neurology clinics of North America. (21), 483-500.

Horne, J. A. (1978). A review of the biological effects of total sleep deprivation in man. Biological Psychology. 7, 55-102.

Jacobi, G.,Reipert, T., Kieslich, M., & Bohl, J. [Fatal outcome during physiotherapy (Vojta's method) in a 3-month old infant. Case report and comments on manual therapy in children]. Klin Padiatr 2001 Mar-Apr;213(2):76-85

Johnson, M. H., Posner, M. I., and Rothbart, M. K., (1991). Components of visual orienting in infancy: Contingnency learning, anticipatory looking and disengaging. Journal of Cognitive Neuroscience, 3, 335-344.

Josefi, O. and Ryan, V. (2004) 'Non-directive play therapy for young children with autism: A case study'. Clinical Child Psychology and Psychiatry, vol. 9, no. 4, pp533-551

Ketelaar, M., Vermeer, A., Hart, H., Petegem-van Beek, E., Helders, P. (2001). Effects of a functional therapy program on motor abilities of children with cerebral palsy. Physical Therapy, 81, 9, 1534-1545.

Kim H, Lee MH, Chang HK, Lee TH, Lee HH, Shin MC, et al. Influence of prenatal noise and music on the spatial memory and neurogenesis in the hippocampus of developing rats. Brain Dev 2006;28:109-14.

Kleitman, N., (1961). The Nature of Dreaming. In, Wolstenholme, G. E. W., and O' Connor, M. (1961). The Nature of Sleep. London. Churchill.

Kleitman, N., (1982). Basic Rest – Activity Cycle. – 22 years later. Sleep, (4), 311-317.

Lewis, M., & Brooks-Gunn, J. (1979). Social cognition and the acquisition of self. New York. Plenum. In Schaffer, H. R.. (1996). Social Development. Oxford. Blackwell.

Liberty, K. (2004) Developmental gains in early intervention based on Conductive Education by young children with motor disorders. International Journal of Rehabilitation Research, 27, 1, 17-25.

Lozanov, G. http://www.cerebromente.org.br/n15/mente/musica.html

Nagaraja D, Jayashree S. Randomized study of the dopamine receptor agonist piribedil in the treatment of mild cognitive impairment. Am J Psychiatry 2001;158:1517-9.

Macey, P. M., Henderson, L. A., Macey, K. E., Alger, J. R., Frysinger, R. C. Woo, M. A., Harper, R. K. Yan-Go, F. L., and Harper, R. M. (2002). Brain Morphology Associated with Obstructive Sleep Apnea. American Journal of Respiratory and Critical Care Medicine. 166: 1382-1387

Marriage, K. J., Gordon, V., and Brand, L. A social skills group for boys with Asperger's syndrome. Australian and New Zealand Journal of Psychiatry. 1995, Vol. 29, No. 1 , Pages 58-62

Marshall, J.C. and Newcombe, F. (1973) Patterns of paralexia: A psycholinguistic approach. Journal of Psycholinguistic Research, 2, 175-199.

Maunsell, J. H. R., and Yang, T. The Effect of Perceptual Learning on Neuronal Responses in Monkey Visual Area V4. The Journal of Neuroscience, February 18, 2004, 24(7):1617-1626;

Mercer, N. (1995). The Guided Construction of Knowledge: Talk amongst teachers and learners. Clevedon. Multilingual Matters.

Mulleners, W. M., Chronicle, E. P., Palmer, J, E., Koehler, P. J., and Vredeveld, J. W. (2001), Suppression of perception in migraine:

Evidence for reduced inhibition in the visual cortex, Neurology, January 23, 2001; 56(2): 178 – 183.

Murray, L., & Trevarthen, C. (1985). Emotional regulation of interactions between two – month olds and their mothers. In Rogoff, B. (1990). Apprenticeship in thinking. Oxford. Oxford University Press.

Palmer, F. B., Shapiro, B. K., Wachtel, R. C., Allen, M. C., Hiller, J. E., Harryman, S. E. Mosher, S. B., Meinert, C. L. and Capute. A. J. The effects of physical therapy on cerebral palsy. A controlled trial in infants with spastic diplegia. New England Journal of Medicine. Volume 318: 803 – 808. March 31 1988 Number13

Pipp, S., Easterbrooks, M. A., & Brown, S. R. (1993). Attachment status and complexity of infants' self and other – knowledge when tested with mother and father. Social Development. 2, 1-14.

Posner, M. I. and Cohen, Y. (1984) Components of visual orienting. In: Attention and Performance: Control of Language Processes, vol 10, Eds H. Bouma, D. Boulshuis. DG Erlbaum: Hillsdale, NJ.

Reddihough et al, 1998, in Law, M. C. Evidence based rehabilitation, a guide to practice. SLACK Incorporated; First edition (30 April 2002)ISBN-10: 1556424531

Rizzo, M. and Robin, D. A. (1990). Simultanagnosia: A defect of sustained attention yields insights on visual information processing. Neurology, 40, 447-455.

Rogoff, B., Malkin, C., and Gilbride, K. (1984). Interaction with babies as guidance in development. In Rogoff, B. (1990). Apprenticeship in Thinking: Cognitive Development in Social Context. Oxford. Oxford University Press.

Rogoff, B. (1990). Apprenticeship in thinking. Oxford. Oxford University Press.

Rogoff, B., Mosier, C., Mistry, J., and Goncu, A. (1993). Toddlers' guided participation with their caregivers in cultural activity. In,

Cultural worlds of early childhood. London & Milton Keynes. Routledge.

Ropper, A. H. and Samuels, M. A. (2000) Adams & Victor's Principles of Neurology, 7th edition McGraw-Hill Professional; 7 edition (December 19, 2000)

Schaffer, H. R.. (1996). Social Development. Oxford. Blackwell

Scherzer, A.L., Mike, V., and Ilson, J. (1976). Physical therapy as a determinant of change in the cerebral palsied infant. Pediatrics. 58. (1). Pp. 47-51

Schück S, Bentué-Ferrer D, Kleinermans D, Reymann JM, Polard E, Gandon JM, et al. Psychomotor and cognitive effects of piribedil, a dopamine agonist, in young healthy volunteers. Fundam Clin Pharmacol 2002;16:57-65.

Sinkkonen J., Tervaniemi M. (2000). Towards optimal recording and analysis of the mismatch negativity. Audio Neurootol. 5, 235–246 doi: 10.1159/000013885. [Cross Ref]

Spiers, H. http://snowdrop-snowdropblog.blogspot.com/2010/09/brain-plasticity-in-action-function.html.

Stepakoff, S., Beebe, B., and Jaffe, J. (2006). Mother-infant tactile communication at four months: http://www.isisweb.org/ICIS2000Program/web_pages/group1039.html

Stern, D. (1985). The interpersonal world of the infant. . In Woodhead, M. Faulkner, D. & Littleton, K. (Eds). (1998). Cultural worlds of early childhood. London and New York. Routledge

Sutton, A. 1989. The impact of conductive education. In Jones, N. ed. Special Education Needs Review. No. 2 pp. 161 – 187.

Särkämö, T., Tervaniemi, M., Laitinen, M., Forsblom, M., Soinila, S, Mikkonen, M., Autti, T, Silvennoinen, H. M., Erkkilä, J., Laine, M., Peretz, I. and Hietanen, M. Music listening enhances cognitive recovery and mood after middle cerebral artery stroke. Brain (2008) 131 (3): 866-876.

Tharp, R. G., and Gallimore, R. (1997). Rousing minds to life: Teaching, learning and schooling in social context. Cambridge. Cambridge University Press.

Thomson, S. M., Fortunato, C., McKinney, R. A., Muller, M., and Gahwiler, B. H. (1996). Mechanisms underlying the neuropathological consequences of epileptic activity in the rat hippocampus in vitro. Journal of Comparative Neurology,372, 515-528.

Tomasello, M. (1995). Joint attention and social cognition. In C. Moore & P. Dunham (Eds.), Joint attention: Its origin and role in development. Hillsdale, NJ: Erlbaum.

Tirosh and Rabino. Physiotherapy for Children With Cerebral Palsy: Evidence for Its Efficacy. Am J Dis Child.1989; 143: 552-555.

Todd, J. E. Conductive Education, the continuing challenge, Physiotherapy, 1990 76 (1) pp13 - 16

Trevarthen, C. (1995). The child's need to learn a culture. Children and Society, 9(1), 1995.

Wood, D., Bruner, J. S., and Ross, G. (1976). The role of tutoring in problem solving. Journal of Child Psychology and Psychiatry. 17(2): 89-100.

Wright, T. and Nicholson, J. (1973). Physiotherapy for the spastic child: - An evaluation. Developmental medicine and child neurology. 15 146-163.

Xu F, Cai R, Xu J, Zhang J, Sun X. Early music exposure modifies GluR2 protein expression in rat auditory cortex and anterior cingulate cortex. Neurosci Lett 2007;420:179-83.

#0457 - 120318 - C0 - 229/152/9 - PB - DID2145325